story of sociology

a first companion to social theory

Gregor McLennan

story of sociology

a first companion to social theory

BLOOMSBURY ACADEMIC

First published in 2011 by:

Bloomsbury Academic
An imprint of Bloomsbury Publishing Plc
36 Soho Square, London W1D 3QY, UK

and

175 Fifth Avenue, New York, NY 10010, USA

CIP records for this book are available from the
British Library and the Library of Congress.
ISBN 978-1-84966-349-6 (paperback)
ISBN 978-1-84966-458-5 (ebook)

This book is produced using paper that is made from
wood grown in managed, sustainable forests.
It is natural, renewable and recyclable. The logging
and manufacturing processes conform to the
environmental regulations of the country of origin.

Printed and bound in Great Britain by the
MPG Books Group, Bodmin, Cornwall.

www.bloomsburyacademic.com

Cover designer: Jim Weaver
Cover image: flowerphotos/Alamy

Contents

Acknowledgements

The themes of this book first found expression in the chapters I contributed to *Exploring Society: Sociology for New Zealand Students*, 3rd edition (McLennan *et al.* 2009). I'm grateful to Ruth McManus, Allanah Ryan, and Paul Spoonley, my co-authors of that text and its previous editions, together with publisher Pearson, for their good will towards this completely re-worked project. Special thanks go to Ruth, who read a full draft of the manuscript and offered valuable suggestions. I am also grateful to two anonymous reviewers, and to my supportive editors Emily Salz and Lee Ann Tutton.

Introduction

This sketch of the history and nature of sociological thinking is offered only as a first companion for students on what ought to be a much longer journey through the landmark writings of the sociological tradition(s), and through the many commentaries written by fellow sociologists that have assisted me in producing this capsule version. And as an introduction, the tale presented here is essentially one about sociological theory, in fact social theory more generally, to some extent. This slant can mislead us into thinking that the research methods, techniques, empirical findings and ethical issues of concrete social investigation are less central than general theorizing. This is not the case, because every social scientist knows that the specifics of research constantly generate new theoretical ideas.

However, it is the ideas that, when grasped, fire up most of us, and these need to be well packaged if students are to be drawn into the subject. *Story of Sociology* seeks to provide that access point for first-year undergraduates studying sociology and related subjects. The book should also enable continuing students to touch base periodically throughout their degree. *Story* might even be a good starting point for taught and research postgraduates, especially those coming into sociology having taken other degrees. The idea is that the book should be slim and approachable enough for readers to delve into it whilst away from their desks and doing other things. Equally, its component chapters can serve as triggers for seminar discussions. Indeed, I am trying to reach seminar leaders (teaching assistants, graduate assistants, tutors, etc.) almost as much as the students they facilitate, because a briefing like this could be helpful for that important animating role. The 'In sum' and 'Interchange' sections at the end of each chapter are intended to help prompt this sense of dialogue between teacher and student.

As to the overall coloration of my narrative, I have chosen to emphasize the early phases of sociological enquiry and current discussions about the nature of the discipline, with the details of the theories and thinkers that come in between given skimpier treatment. This is partly just for reasons of economy, given that readers are likely to return to the latter, whereas following first encounter, the founding questions and thinkers are sometimes left to lie in the background. But also, since my treatment of sociology has more of a social-theory slant than a narrowly disciplinary one, it is the type of conceptual and cultural questioning shared by forebears and contemporaries alike that I want to underline – not least because the very idea of sociology announced in that earlier epoch is under significant re-examination from many angles today.

In terms of the overarching perspective that informs the narrative, my view is that sociology is rendered viable and significant only as a critical-progressivist and secular approach, both to social understanding and to our common political futures. But not only must such an orientation be tempered by reflexivity and complexity, my approach to teaching has always given students plenty of space and encouragement to develop their own views, including opposition to mine.

1

Why sociology?

Let's start with some very basic issues about what motivates us to choose to study a particular subject at university.

Instrumental and intrinsic motivations

One pressing consideration is the extent to which it might assist you in gaining useful employment. Indeed, listening to some government officials and newspaper pundits, you might think that this is just about the only motivation for expending large fees on advanced education (or accruing substantial debt because of it). The assumption is that there is a direct correlation between undergraduate degree pathways and a secure, affluent trajectory through the world of work. However, sociological observation reveals this to be a questionable assumption. For one thing, the labour market – like everything else in today's 'fast capitalism' – can be very flexible, volatile and short-term: specialist skills and credentials need to be gained and updated 'on the job' rather than in formal education, and well-qualified graduates in many subjects often wait years before embarking on what previous generations might regard as a proper career. In any case, that job track may well turn out to be shorter than expected, with career jumps becoming quite common, whether driven by choice or necessity. Partly as a result of this, it is postgraduate qualifications that are seen as necessary for entering specialized and well-paid vocations. Most employers of first-degree graduates just want people who are adaptable and who can think.

If this might seem a rather humdrum and even dispiriting way to begin an overview of social theory, the message is important: that even when we think instrumentally about what we might get out of higher education, we need to think sociologically about the real state of the world and our personal place in it. And we need to make the firm choice to enter our field of study primarily on intrinsic grounds, not (primarily) for instrumental reasons. As it happens, there are good instrumental reasons for taking up the critical social sciences. In the previous generation, these subjects were regarded, employment-wise, as the ones to take if you wanted to become be a lecturer, social worker, prison educational officer and the like. This is still the case, because such people-centred, education-driven work remains extremely valuable. And with pressures to maintain 'work-life balance' in the face of demanding output and performance expectations, sociologically-minded intermediaries are needed to manage and facilitate people, attuned as they are to appreciating where everyone is 'coming from' in terms of their background identities and aspirations.

In addition, we also now live in societies in which the supply, interpretation and use of information are far more pervasive than they used to be. This hugely increases and spreads the face value of the two central sociological aptitudes: researching (finding out) and theorizing (analysing). The 'information society' is positively awash with concepts and facts, and it takes people with good critical judgement to decide which current sources are best fit for purpose, and able themselves to produce valid concepts and data. Researchers and analysts, consequently, have become core roles in all manner of public and private organizations. So it turns out after all that sociology delivers the basis for a wide range of knowledge-society, people-centred occupations.

However, to reiterate, the principal reasons for studying sociology are intrinsic ones – the opening up of critical insight, participation in the power of ideas, the capacity to analyse and manipulate data, and acquisition of sound knowledge of the social world. Paradoxically, in fact, when you pursue something of intrinsic value, this automatically generates pragmatic advantages. To put it facetiously, you don't choose to play the piano in order to rapidly chop up vegetables in a restaurant, but being a good pianist automatically equips you with the generic skills that allow you to take up that particular occupation (and many others).

Just from a purely personal point of view, sociology facilitates self-knowledge and self-development. For people who have just left school, sociology provides a deeper understanding of the contemporary social world. For more mature students, sociology gives intellectual shape to the considerable practical and reflective knowledge that has already been acquired in real life. Sociology enhances self-understanding partly by challenging the common-sense assumptions that are passed down the line to us, whether through our families, peers, dominant elites or the mass media. The result of critically engaging with common-sense influences on us — sometimes sound enough, sometimes rather appalling — is frequently liberating. But sociology is not only about self-development; it is not a 'selfish' subject at all. What it consistently demonstrates is that our individual situations and fate are closely and inextricably bound up with those of others. Some of these others are seemingly 'people like us', but many are also (apparently) very different, and sociologists seek to understand these different social relations in order to grasp what makes everyone tick.

Sociology also helps us comprehend and shape systemic social change. A memorable slogan of one of the classic figures of sociology, Karl Marx, was that the point of study and thinking was not only to interpret the world, but to change it. Sociology was born in the heat of a changing modern world around 200 years ago, and it constantly forces us to think about whether society is progressing or not; about who are the winners and losers of social change; about whose side we are on; and about how things can be changed for the better. Sociology is thus intimately bound up with questions of social justice and attracts the sort of people who care about social justice. It helps us make our way in the world, but it also makes us see what it is about the nature and direction of society that enables people to make it out there (or not) in the ways that they do.

Initial definitions

In his mega-textbook, Anthony Giddens (Giddens 2006: 4) describes our subject in the following way:

> Sociology is the scientific study of human social life, groups and societies. It is a dazzling and compelling enterprise, as its subject matter is our own behaviour as social beings. The scope of sociological study is extremely wide, ranging from the analysis of passing encounters between individuals on the street to the investigation of global social processes.

This depiction usefully signals that sociology is a kind of scientific discipline: like other sciences, sociology takes a distinctive subject matter for analysis, one that represents an independent and complex reality, and it produces systematic knowledge about this reality, rather than merely subjective opinion. But Giddens's definition also summons up the subjective side of things, that is, our personal experience of society as lived from the inside. Sociology is 'dazzling' and 'compelling' to us — whether or not we can say it produces correct knowledge as such. And the 'scope of sociological study is extremely wide' — so wide, in fact, that a multitude of topic areas can be covered and a multitude of points of view can be debated. In sociology, little is ruled out as necessarily wrong, and no views, not even scientific views, are sacred. So whilst sociologists do strive to ensure that their work is as thorough, and in that sense as impartial, as it can be, sociology is conducted by people who are already involved in what they study, and are part of it. Sociology probably cannot, then, ever be a wholly disinterested enterprise, if by that we mean seeking to attain a 'God's-eye view' of the world. We can reach towards objectivity as far as possible, but in sociology there will always be much scope for moral and political debate and attachment.

Defenders of pure objectivity – such people are not usually practising scientists, by the way – sometimes tell us that the facts speak for themselves. But, in fact, facts never speak for themselves: they always have to be interpreted to take on any significance. And interpretation always involves not only theorizing, but imagination and empathy as well – thus one of the catchphrases of our discipline: the sociological imagination. The originator of this phrase was C. Wright Mills, an American sociologist working in the 1950s and 1960s, and his message still resonates. Mills emphasized that what we often experience as private troubles in life – unemployment, relationship difficulties, stress, apathy, aggression and so on – need to be seen not primarily as personal matters, but rather as public issues: things to be explored and debated as definite social phenomena. Mills (Mills 1959: 6–7) went on to pose some of the questions that sociologists ask in arriving at any satisfactory big picture:

- ▸ What is the structure of this particular society as a whole?
- ▸ What are its essential components, and how are they related to one another?
- ▸ Where does this society stand in human history?
- ▸ What varieties of men and women now prevail in this society and in this period?
- ▸ In what ways are they 'selected and formed, liberated and repressed, made sensitive and blunted?'

These questions are demanding as well as fascinating. Any answers to them require us to describe and conceptualize the basic features of our social world, to put the latter in historical context, and to grasp the ethical and political dimensions and consequences of the current social order. They also raise a central methodological matter in sociology: the relationship between empirical observation and theoretical generalization.

Observation, methods and theory

Let's pursue this relationship by thinking about rioting. Rioting often appears to people – especially people in privileged groups, in the media and in government – as shocking, unnecessary, mindless and deviant. In conservative newspapers and other forms of media, riots are often vividly represented and pigeon-holed as basically criminal: the irresponsible acts of bad people who should take up whatever personal troubles they have in a more constructive and patient way, rather than turn them into public issues in this violent, useless way. Sociologists, however, need to take a more considered approach (which does not necessarily mean condoning riotous violence as such), looking for the deeper social causes of violent and apparently random disturbances, and also working out some of the social complexities behind apparently simple and inconsiderate behaviour such as looting, burning and throwing dangerous missiles.

Take one of the most extensive and dramatic urban upheavals of the late twentieth century, the Los Angeles (LA) riots of April 1992. Fifty-five people died in these disturbances,

2,000 were injured, 12,000 arrested, hundreds of businesses and buildings were burned to the ground, and very graphic scenes of violence and looting were beamed into living rooms all around the world as the story unfolded. Indeed, in an important sense, the LA riots were a media event, a mediated event. The initial incident that triggered the disorder, the beating by police of an African-American man, Rodney King, was caught on a personal video camera by a passer-by. This clip was then represented on the main TV networks, and tension mounted in the streets. The trial of the white officers involved was also shown on TV, and the riots were begun by people standing outside TV shops in their LA neighbourhoods who surged with anger when they saw that the officers had been acquitted. We know this because more TV cameras were filming those people watching the TV trial. Thereafter, nightly scenes of the blazing, ripping events were represented to the world at large. This sparked off further rioting in other US cities.

Throughout the whole process, from the initial incident to the sombre aftermath, a huge sequence of experts, protagonists and ordinary people were wheeled in front of the viewers to give an account of their own feelings about who or what was to blame, and their proposed remedies. The events were all too real, but so were the *representations* of the events, and the different sorts of 'representations of representations', whether on TV or in the analyses of the various commentators.

Indeed, we need to wonder whether the considerable shock around the LA riots stems in part from an outsider viewpoint that has built up a perverse but pervasive image of LA itself. Home to countless celebrities and millionaires, its wealth built out of the manufacture of images and stories that we almost take for real (our familiar Disney friends, etc.), 'LA – the image' in turn feeds into a more general Disneyfied, fantastical view of what America as a whole is like. The LA riots were in that sense a significant wake-up call for anyone inclined to let the dazzle of glitzy capitalism screen out the more grinding everyday reality of most people's lives in that city.

To understand the LA unrest sociologically therefore involves coming to terms with a lot of hard facts: the numbers of people dead or wounded, the numbers arrested, the figures for property damage and so on. There is also the need to find out about the full range of representations mentioned above. How did the police see it, how did the President see it, how did the shopkeepers see it, how did the black youths see it? Was there a Latino point of view that was different from that of black people? Were any white people involved? Was there a discrepancy between the accounts of African-American and Korean-American people? (There was tension and some conflict between these two groups.) Did Americans generally think that the trial of the officers who beat Rodney King was fair? And what about the respective gender roles and the views of women across and between these different groups, given that confrontational street action tends to be conducted by men?

In addition to these facts relating to the events and to perspectives on them, there are important background data to get a grip of: what were the trends in income and employment levels amongst African-Americans in LA in the period leading up to the disturbances? Were the drop-out and truancy rates in schools increasing? What is the evidence of prior police racism or heavy-handedness? Does the record show that US justice is consistently fair to black Americans? Do black Americans think they get fair justice? What does a comparison between the situations and views of black, Latino and Korean people in LA reveal?

You can see here that sociologists have plenty to research, and there are different research methods we need to use. For example, if we want to know how many people died in the LA disturbances, or what property was destroyed, or what the extent of previous social deprivation was, we can collect and work through the relevant documentary sources (death certificates, police statistics, fire department damage assessment reports, school records, employment statistics and indices of housing and living standards). If we want to know what various groups of people thought about what happened and its significance, we could go and talk to them in interviews in order to get a better view. However, we can't talk to everyone, so we might design a questionnaire that a large number of people might be prepared to fill in and return. This would give us more aggregate information but, probably, not terribly rich information. To get that, we could seek access into one of the local communities, spending a significant amount of time getting to know some people, observing them and discussing with them at length their life history, their community characteristics, their attitudes to authority, their hopes and fears. This kind of in-depth personal exchange, designed to develop in the sociologist a close-up feel for a particular way of life and reflected in reports that give a voice to those being studied, is usually referred to as ethnography.

If we wanted to understand the pressures the police feel in situations such as the LA riots, we might temporarily join up with the police, or follow them around, to try to get a sense of their motivations and perceptions – and even to just find out what they do on the streets. This kind of research is sometimes known as participant observation.

If we wanted to know how often items of news and comment on the riots appeared in the media, and the coloration of editorial opinion, we might collect all the relevant newspapers for the period and work out the column inches devoted to the subject, as compared with other subjects. We could then work out a scale of measurement to summarize the editorial values of the main papers towards the events. We could do a similar exercise on the importance of the events in terms of TV-time (this involves what is called content analysis). We would also want to give attention to the subtle ways in which the images and words that were published in the media to represent the riots – whether intentionally or unintentionally – conveyed a particular political or moral slant. Working like this on the meanings of the 'texts' of the riots – statements, interviews, reports, images, commentaries, testimonies – is known as the semiotics of sociological research.

In trying to understand what happened, and why, in LA, 1992, we have to ask general questions about the relationship between social violence, social conditions, the prevalence and impact of racism, and the role of the media in shaping or disseminating information about society and its defining events. We are asking about what goes on when differences amongst people take the form of serious social divisions and major clashes of group interest/belonging. To comprehend particular events, we need general concepts such as, in this case, racism, poverty and multiculturalism, but the particular exemplification of those concepts in turn qualifies them further. There is a constant tacking between the general and the particular, and 'middle range' concepts are part of this – we may need to talk, for example, about the formation of a 'black underclass' or an 'African-Korean petit bourgeoisie' to help see why different groups in similar areas of the same city reacted differently. Theoretical labelling, therefore, is indispensable, if only to develop working hypotheses – interesting and plausible propositions that may or may not turn out to be right. Such labelling is frequently controversial. Think, for example, of the different connotations of calling what happened in LA a 'criminal riot' as against 'social disorder', or an 'urban uprising', or even a 'political rebellion'. On their own, the facts don't tell us decisively which set of concepts is most appropriate, but they help test the value of theories, just as theories endow the facts with sociological meaning. Theories act as interpretations that direct us to certain sorts of evidence, and the evidence in turn helps us to fine-tune the theories and concepts.

What, then, is theory? Theory comes into play whenever we wish to explain something, or to describe something by devising an unexpected terminology for it. Theory involves developing concepts and arguments which answer 'why' questions ('Why did that happen?', 'Why is there racism?') and 'what' questions ('What sort of social phenomenon is a riot?').

Theory is indispensable for getting us to think about the deep significance of the things by abstracting from the countless particular features of a situation to try to get to the essential forces and relationships at work within them. It is commonly assumed that just because theorizing involves abstraction, it leads to impenetrable jargon that only academics produce. This is wrong. Language itself is kind of everyday theoretical toolkit – the word-concept 'dog', for example, abstracts from and includes every particular Rover, Sheba, Patch and Lassie that exists. Actually, we theorize all the time in our ordinary lives. In their own minds, and with friends, people thrash out various ideas and hypotheses concerning why their relationship broke down, why they became unemployed, why they dislike some people or are themselves disliked by others. And all subcultures, not just academic ones, have their own favoured, apparently impenetrable jargon.

An important staging post on the way from the particular to the general (and back again) is by way of sociological comparison, both historically and across different social situations. The LA riots had many unique features, but some of the same fundamental processes (to do with racism and urban deprivation – the intersection of race and class, in other words) can be observed in an earlier LA riot in 1965, known as the Watts riots. Or if we want to focus on how rioting itself raises consciousness of poverty and oppression, such that we even want to call certain types of riot 'uprisings', it would not be absurd to draw out some similarities between LA in 1965/1992 and the storming of the Bastille in Paris in 1789, the event that sparked the first great social revolution of modern times, the French Revolution, from which stemmed our whole modern vocabulary of equality and social justice. But if 1789 and even 1992 feel like a long time ago, we can bring more recent riots into the picture, such as those in the north of England in 2001 in cities like Bradford (no deaths, 300 arrests), those in the outskirts of Paris, Lyon and over a hundred other towns in France in 2005 (1 death, 9,000 burnt vehicles, 3,000 arrests), and even perhaps the strident student demonstrations in London in 2010–11.

In sum

The example I have used – the LA riots of 1992 – may not ring many bells with readers too young to recall them. But the point of the discussion was not to share common experiences with you. Even if I had chosen more recent stormy events (and their aftermaths), such as the attacks by Islamicists on the Twin Towers in New York on 11 September 2001 or the social meaning of Hurricane Katrina in New Orleans in August 2005, the momentous feelings that everyone has when confronted with the immediacy of such episodes inevitably fades, so that any cases that are chosen to be sociologically exemplary soon come to seem dated. The point is rather that when further social disturbances of this sort occur – and they can be expected with some confidence – they will need to be sociologically analysed along the same sort of lines as the LA riots of 1992. Moreover, in that sociological analysis, our immediate emotional and political reaction, the sociological research that begins to put them into proper context, and theoretical explanations and framings that ultimately make sense of the events, are very closely interlinked. This is the intrinsic value and promise of sociological understanding.

Interchange

Question:

Giddens's definition of sociology was a bit of a mouthful. Do you have a better one?

Response:

Shorter, rather than better:

Sociology is the study of social systems, institutions, interactions and ideologies.

2

Sociology as understanding modernity

Sociology came into being as an intellectual response to the rapidly changing social world of late eighteenth- and early nineteenth-century Europe. These historical roots still inform the focus and content of the discipline and some of the basic features of that world are still with us today. The label customarily given to the whole period from then to the end of the twentieth century is modernity. And the single biggest debate in sociology for the past thirty years has been about whether, in our time, we have experienced a major shift out of the societal epoch of modernity and into one that is significantly different, postmodernity for short. This is a powerful image, as if we have been collectively bestriding two gigantic tectonic plates of history and society.

The modernity-versus-postmodernity issue raises another one, concerning whether it is a good thing for sociologists to be continually absorbed with such tectonic or epochal or totalizing concerns. Instead of continually defining and debating such polarized and all-purpose terms, shouldn't we be researching and theorizing much more specific things – bits of the world and particular episodes, rather than the whole thing, which can probably never be settled anyway? So, as well as finding different types of 'totalizers' amongst social theorists, you also find various kinds of 'interceptors' and 'downscalers'. Interceptors like to shoot down grand theories, almost just for the sake of it, while downscalers like to show that, on the ground, things look much less all of a piece than they do from on high.

The central concept

On the totalizing side of things, modernity means the kind of society that is:

▸ industrial rather than pre- or post-industrial;
▸ capitalist, rather than feudal, slave-based or socialist in economic structure;
▸ urban rather than rural;
▸ socially and psychologically dynamic and mobile rather than static;
▸ dominated by the nation state as a form of political integration;
▸ individualistic rather than based on traditional tribes or castes;
▸ secular rather than religious;
▸ liberal and democratic in political ideology;
▸ a mass society, in terms of access to basic goods and rights.

Just to be clear: part of the reason for talking in terms of a story of sociology, rather than, say, the facts of social and sociological development, is that in using such terms as modernity and postmodernity, we are *reconstructing* a history by reference to its projected tendencies or imputed patterns. And almost every component of these reconstructions is debatable in some way. Thus, from the interceptor's point of view, we might want to query whether some of those listed traits do actually distinguish modern societies from older or later ones. Perceptions of social and psychological 'dynamism', for example, are strongly culturally relative and often very subjective. A downscaler might add that some of the allegedly uniform traits listed – democracy, urbanization and mass access to goods and rights, for instance – only become prevalent, if they do at all, very late on in the supposedly modern period. And even totalizing sociologists might disagree about which traits of modernity are most important. Some assert that the fundamental feature of modernity is capitalism, others that it is industrialism, whilst others again point to the development of the nation state.

There is also an issue about whether the very concept of modernity itself is fundamentally Eurocentric, seeing as it appears to extrapolate from the historical experience of just a handful of West European countries and project it on to the global social world as a whole. For these reasons and more besides, books and articles have been written with titles like 'We Have Never Been Modern' and 'Against Modernity', and increasingly today the preference is to talk about 'multiple modernities' rather than modernity in the singular.

That said, both the concept of modernity, and the proposition that sociology is in some central way about understanding modernity, remain heuristically viable. That is, they serve as a constructive line of thinking, something to be tried out and refined through continual bouts of affirmation and critique. They also help us direct attention to the component phases and structural subdivisions of modernity, because we don't get far in our talk of modernity without finding ourselves talking about early or late modernity, or about how the different dimensions of modernity operate and relate to one another – notably its socio-economic, political and cultural dimensions.

Putting together these considerations about the phases of modernity and its structural subdivisions, it is convenient to think about modernity as having first consolidated in the wake of three breakthrough processes: the Industrial Revolution (1780–1840 = socio-economic dimension), the French Revolution (1789–1804 = political dimension), and the Enlightenment as intellectual revolution (1730s–1800 = cultural dimension).

Socio-economic transformation

The Industrial Revolution has been described as the most far-reaching transformation in humanity's existence, at least as recorded in written documents. Yet this momentous episode was initially based in just one trade (cotton manufacturing), in just one part (Lancashire) of just one country (England). We have to be careful here: no profound social development is completely unprecedented or counts as evidence for something uniquely special about the places or peoples from which it derives. Thus, the resources that allowed Britain's take-off into modernity stemmed partly from the proceeds of its overseas colonial empire, and the raw cotton itself was grown in India and the slave-worked plantations of America and the West Indies. So our analysis of Britain's important role in initiating socio-economic modernity should not be understood as judgementally positive.

The industrial formation of the UK growth towns rapidly stimulated national and worldwide markets for a whole range of new commercial and capital goods during the nineteenth century, and a powerful – and threatening – form of social organization came into being, featuring new technologies of industrial production and new social collectivities. The societal landscape was populated by numerous factories, mills, mines, railroads and iron ships; and by factory workers or 'hands' living closely packed lives in tenement or back-to-back housing, all clustered under the smoke of the tall chimneys, amidst a soundscape of hissing steam, clattering machinery and the clamorous voices of a multitude thrown together in unprecedented forms of labour, interaction and experience. Some of those drawn in their droves to the growing cities led a precarious existence, and they responded in opportunistic ways. The governing elites and urban authorities soon became concerned to police this 'dangerous', 'unrespectable' underclass, constructing factory-like prisons in which they might learn some bourgeois discipline, and – following the squalid environment and high mortality rates produced by the opening spell of capitalist industrialism – putting into place elementary sanitation, factory and educational regimes to ensure a suitably routine-based and minimally hygienic way of life.

Even such a dramatic shift in social relations as this took time, so we shouldn't think that older and other forms of life and labour (rural communities, for example) did not carry on within the new industrial capitalist context. Additionally, when spreading out, these processes never take the same form, or occupy the same time span, in different countries. Coming later in the process sometimes enables particular societies to leapfrog over those who were first on the scene. Thus, Germany, for example, came to industrialization later than Britain, but developed higher tech industrial methods more rapidly. This pattern of catch-up, overlap and overtake can readily be noticed in the present time, in the way that China and India today are pushing forward with certain aspects of industrialization, some of them very like early industrial Britain, others being platformed through the latest electronic, biotechnological and nano-engineering developments.

Apart from the first breakthrough into modernity, sociologists have identified a number of subsequent phases in the socio-economic dimension. That initial phase was characterized, for example, by industrial capital being raised directly by individuals and families, such that (male) heads of household were the principal beneficiaries of the profits derived, and the latter widely viewed as the legitimate rewards for personal effort and enterprise. There was also a strong element of paternalism and philanthropy in the way that the condition of the workers and the poor was regarded and ameliorated. This personalized model of the free-market or liberal industrial economy progressively then gave way to a more impersonal, multi-stranded one. Just as modernity as a whole tends to experience a certain split between economy, culture and politics, so, within the socio-economic dimension itself, internal differentiation occurs. Thus, different sectors of industry proliferate and operate according to their own logic – agriculture, producer goods, consumption goods, service provision, luxury markets, leisure commodities, financial services and banking in all its aspects. Family proprietors join together to form larger corporations, and cartels amongst those corporations emerge.

On the labour side, trade unions and groups of unions consolidate. Ownership both concentrates and yet also dilutes as the operation and investment of capital funds becomes the task of managers who increasingly lack direct ownership and control of productive assets, or are guaranteed a direct share in profits. Rather, they make their living by way of a salary for putting assets to work and for running teams in manufacture, distribution and service. Marxist sociologists depict this phase as a kind of 'mature' or high state of capitalism, predicting that capitalism cannot long remain the creation of individual Victorian entrepreneurs, but rather that of a massive, increasingly international and institutional system of property investment and labour exploitation. Theorists of the 'managerial revolution' in the 1920s and 1930s took the opposite view: capitalism had become an inappropriate term for a technological society of experts, managers and middle-men of all sorts.

One influential label for large-scale, systemic and organized industrial society in this mode is Fordism. This term pulls together the idea of (capitalist) modernity as a mass society of production and consumption, driven according to 'scientific management' principles based upon time-and-motion studies of workplace efficiency. It generates a huge degree of sameness in citizens based around our common desire for, and increasing achievement of, commodities – symbolized iconically by the first Model T Ford (1913) and then subsequently by fridges, TVs, package holidays, web access, insurance policies, privately owned housing and the rest. In Fordist ideology and Fordist economic strategy, we all live the same sorts of lives; aspire to the same material things; get used to a steady rhythm of (heterosexual, monogamous) domestic existence and workplace routine; and this is all generally regarded as a very good thing – because it is a positive, modern thing.

Modern nationhood

What about the political dimension of (European) modernity? Although they may seem utterly familiar to us now, both the nation state and the idea of liberal democracy were forged in early modernity and contribute strikingly to modernity's very definition. The modern concept of the state was first clearly articulated in the Treaty of Westphalia in 1648, though not pursued consistently until the nineteenth century. According to this, the government of a society is the expression of a singular sovereign power operating within a territorially demarcated country, exercising a monopoly of force. This was a novel situation because in many societies prior to that time, there could be co-existing jurisdictions and on-the-ground rivalries between alternative administrative and armed authorities. These forces would derive their mandate from different sources: the will of God, the authority of the Pope, the Church, the Empire, the lord of the manor, popular custom and regional practice. So the exercise of power was often a patchwork affair, re-ordered by the Westphalian system which articulated an overarching system of states, each of which was to possess a political and national personality, so to speak. Instead of the emperor or king being sovereign, it is the state itself, or the government acting in the name of the country, that has agency and rightful control. States, like people, are thought to have the right of self-determination and must therefore be careful to distinguish between internal matters, over which they alone have control, and foreign affairs, where the authority of other states must be acknowledged.

The very idea of a bounded society takes firmer shape in this political context; societies become identified with nation states and particular countries. By the same token, the modern state gets its basic rationale from being the container most suited to the development of modern industrial society. Then, the typical internal sociological features of a national society can be better identified and regulated – its typical forms of economy, religion, education, family socialization, political activism, sporting rituals and so on. And by comparing further what varies and what differs across nations, a more generalized conception of types of society emerges, as does the abstract idea of society as a whole.

The French Revolution did not start or finish this process by which societies became 'statized' or nationalized, but it undoubtedly stands as its distinctive symbolic representation. This is because the French Revolution brought into being the first modern nation state in ideology as well as in territoriality and administrative organization. The slogan 'Liberty, Equality, Fraternity!' was an unprecedented rallying call, encapsulating the idea of genuine popular sovereignty, that is to say, a state and a nation defined by its people, and its people defined by the absence of rank and privilege among individuals. Of course, none of this happened naturally. The formation of the French nation, like many others following in its path, was very much a process of active construction, and even invention. Peasants, it has been said, had to be *made* into Frenchmen, and many of them in fact joined the counter-revolutionary uprisings because they did not want to become Frenchmen in the modern sense. All this alerts us to the fact that modern nations are what historians call 'imagined communities'.

In sum

Although some social theorists have rejected the idea, and whilst almost everyone understands it as an interpretative construct rather than an actual historical reality as such, modernity has been, and remains today, the central concept of sociology. The logic and character of modernity is typically elaborated by focusing on its various component dimensions, notably the socio-economic, the political and the cultural.

Interchange

Question:

You said that these three main dimensions of modern society are related to one another, but also imply that they are separate. How does this work exactly, and which dimension is the most important in how social change happens?

Response:

These are two of the core questions in sociological theory, and they continue to tax and divide sociologists. There are theorists who favour the priority of socio-economic factors, while others promote the centrality of the cultural or the political. These are preferences that one develops for oneself over time, and they are strongly influenced by one's moral and political views on how society operates and what, if anything, is wrong with it. It's not that there is no objective evidence to show which dimension is primary, or which came first – it's just that no amount of evidence is likely to be completely decisive in resolving the issue. This does not leave us floundering: it helps, for example, to think of our different dimensions as the component threads in a cord of rope. Each is separate, but utterly entwined around the others in a constantly spiralling motion, and together they make up the (moving) structure as a whole.

3

Legacies of Enlightenment

We can now pick up on the third factor in the onset of modernity, the cultural revolution known as the Enlightenment, which gripped the minds of teachers, writers, bureaucrats and merchants in many European cities in the course of the eighteenth century. In one sense, the Enlightenment was a quintessentially 'idealist' phenomenon: its philosophers, economists and sociologists felt that if only we could latch on to the right sort of ideas, then we could produce a more rational, free, humanistic and in that sense modern society. And the inspiring ideas of the time were reason, science and progress. Enlightenment ideas did not drop from the skies, however. They were the expression of a social movement and a reflection of larger social processes already under way. This was the period, for example, during which a hugely expanded public sphere of learning and discussion emerged in Europe; when salons and coffee houses, libraries and journals, learned academies, Royal Societies, newspapers and public lectures started to thrive, breaking through the old system of the *ancien régime* in which the production and dissemination of thought had depended upon the sponsorship of individual aristocrats. But now, in a rapidly growing mercantile and commercial economy requiring greater numbers of educated people to do its counting, reading, law-making and trading, educated people became excited by, and organized around, the scientific possibilities of the age: remedies for plagues and diseases, improvements to agricultural methods, inventions of industrial machines and, as well, brand new accounts of the development of what they called civil society.

Knowledge directly spurred human progress, it was believed, and came in two main varieties: knowledge of the natural world and knowledge of human nature itself, which had a socially plastic side to it. For such knowledge to develop and lead the society, the received wisdom and inherited authority of lords and clerics had to be pointedly downgraded. Few Enlightenment thinkers were outright atheists – and quite a few were clergymen – but the traditional style and status of religious thinking, in particular, was thoroughly questioned. In its place stood the ideal of personal autonomy and the need to approach every argument from first principles, worked out under the authority of logic, evidence and imagination. In this spirit, intellectual and moral liberation was thought to be breaking through, following centuries of darkness.

What did the European Enlightenment bequeath to the sociological thinking that rapidly developed in its wake? This can best be addressed by pointing up a number of theoretical (philosophical, political, ethical) tensions lying at the heart of Enlightenment thought, and still very much present in many social theory discussions today.

Science and morals

Isaac Newton was a hero of the Enlightenment, and science was the main thing that brought enlightenment, piercing through the murky clouds of ignorance and unquestioning habit. What was needed for understanding both nature and society was systematic knowledge, knowledge without presuppositions, of the sort exemplified above all by science. However, some Enlighteners felt that the primary goals of knowledge were moral understanding and moral improvement, which were not subject to necessary and constant laws in the way that nature was. So, two different impulses were at work, producing two different models for social study and social criticism. On the one hand, there was scientism – the idea that human history, morality and society could be understood as a matter of objective necessity, providing sure guidelines for social criticism (as the Marquis de Condorcet, for one, believed). On the other hand, there was moralism – the idea that the moral life could not be a subject for science and that 'reason is, and ought only to be, the slave of the passions' (David Hume).

Rationalism and empiricism

Rationalism is a top-down theory of how human knowledge works. It holds that the influence of our previous ideologies and self-interests can be corrected if we rigorously put them under the microscope of pure reason and first principles. In terms of social theory, the rationalist view would be that we can aspire to an objective account of what the core structures of any society are at a given time, and how society has developed as a whole over time. Empiricism, by contrast, is the bottom-up view that nothing can be established by reason alone, and that careful empirical observation can often surprise and offend our sense of reason as well as refute ingrained beliefs. Science, then, including the science of society, is not so much about the speculations of theorists; rather, it is the painstaking accumulation of facts and observations. In a nutshell, rationalism says: 'Work it out.' Empiricism says: 'Look and see.'

Universalism and relativism

The Enlighteners aspired to universality in both their particular theories and their broader intellectual values. If science and reason were to be taken as the lights of progress, this must be because they constitute universally valid benchmarks – guidelines that are true quite generally, regardless of time, place or culture. Yet the Enlighteners were also willing to accept a large degree of relativism, a way of thinking that was familiar to them from ancient Greek philosophy. For relativists, the things that we hold to be objectively and universally true are valid only in the context of the norms and conditions (including physical-geographical conditions) of the environments from which they spring.

The West and the Rest

The place of the Enlightenment was Europe, and its writers believed that their commercial society was more 'advanced' than the supposedly primitive societies that were increasingly coming to its attention through many voyages of 'discovery' of 'new worlds' in that era. As the anthropological reports from these explorations came through, so the mapping of human society itself was constructed according to a scheme of progressive development. It was felt that although savage societies were 'noble' in many ways, they would eventually have to become like those of Europe. This hierarchical scenario, underwritten by science, helped legitimate the political, economic and military process of colonialism. Few of the leading Enlighteners were viciously racist, at least by the standards of the time. In fact, their appreciation of the diversity and value of the expanded range of human societies now unfolding before their eyes was deep and genuine. Diderot, one of the main compilers of the famous first *Encyclopedie*, urged the Tahitian islanders to protect themselves against the voyagers from Europe, because one day, he said, they will come with crucifix in one hand and a dagger in the other, 'to cut your throats or to force you to accept their customs and opinions'. Still, the majority of Enlightenment intellectuals had little doubt that the natives of the 'Rest' were morally and factually inferior to the sophisticated denizens of the 'West'.

Men and women

The Enlightenment claimed to speak for all humanity, and its guiding concern was summarized in a poem by Alexander Pope: 'the proper study of Mankind is Man'. But to epitomize the Enlightenment in this way immediately poses the question:

where do women come into the picture? The answer is that they don't, very much. Many highly intellectual women were involved in the social movement of the Enlightenment, but they tended to be the wives and mistresses of the more renowned male thinkers, and played the role of the hostesses of the salons where lots of exciting discussions between the men – and sometimes the women, too – took place. Even if subordinated to the thinking men at the time, there were certainly more women, and more important women thinkers, actively involved than history-writing, until recently, has permitted us to grasp. Mary Wollstonecraft (1759–97), for one, has been steadily upgraded over time into a thinker of high standing, and other early feminist writers and thinkers are being (re-)discovered all the time. Wollstonecraft's remarkable *A Vindication of the Rights of Women* shows how difficult it was in the Age of Reason to get a feminist agenda going. On the one hand, she felt the need to be as rigorously rational as a man (because she *was*) in making the case for the extension to women of male rights of freedom and equality in all spheres of life and thought. But Wollstonecraft remained unapologetic about contesting injustices against women in an impassioned tone. She was among the first to insist that the very split between rational argument (and public life), on the one hand, and the emotional life (along with domestic/parenting values), on the other, was a form of patriarchal manipulation. Of course, Enlightenment men could then sidestep Wollstonecraft's challenge on the grounds that it was rather too emotional.

Radicalism and reformism

We have been talking about a single Enlightenment, but, although the key ideas of reason, science, and progress were widely shared, the movement consolidated into a serious struggle between an intellectually and politically cautious tendency, and a distinctively more radical one. The former was content to leave the business of illumination and critique to the life of the mind; they did not push the campaign against falsity, inherited wealth and social privilege too far; and they generally felt that the French Revolution, when it came, was extremist and retrograde. The radical Enlightenment thinkers, by contrast, were philosophical materialists, holding that humans were an interesting sort of animal or machine, whose mental and spiritual capacities could not be viewed as standing apart from their physical and social environments. These writers were also prepared to commit themselves wholeheartedly to the cause of greater egalitarianism and held hopes for the perfection of humanity. From this point of view, the French Revolution, though perhaps unpleasant and flawed, was a necessary step in the right direction.

Sameness and difference

As a tradition of thought, sociology has been wrapped up in all these tensions that the Enlightenment has handed down the line. Indeed, it is quite remarkable, given the time that has passed, that some of the hottest debates in sociology today continue to replay many of these Enlightenment issues and oppositions. For example, we are nowadays preoccupied by questions of social and cultural identity, and the need to fully recognize the profound differences between groups and individuals in terms of their ethnicity, class, gender, sexuality and culture. Sometimes the argument is put forward that mainstream sociologists seek, in the name of a generalized humanity that is all the same, to suppress the troubling extent of the myriad crucial differences in identity and culture. In the light of this contemporary dilemma, it is instructive to consider how one of the forerunners of sociology, John Millar of Glasgow University, tackled this kind of issue in the early 1770s:

> When we contemplate the amazing diversity to be found in the laws of different countries, and even of the same country at different periods, our curiosity is naturally excited to enquire in what manner mankind have been led to embrace such different rules of conduct … In searching for the causes of those peculiar systems of law and government which have appeared in the world, we must undoubtedly resort, first of all, to the differences of situation which have suggested different views and motives of action to the inhabitants of particular countries … The variety that frequently occurs in these and such other particulars, must have a prodigious influence upon the great body of a people; as, by giving a peculiar direction to their inclinations and pursuits, it must be productive of correspondent habits, dispositions, and ways of thinking.

In this passage, Millar seems to have no difficulty accepting that the differences between social groups are both fascinating and central. He also mentions a number of things that make up these differences – situation, law, government, rules of conduct, views, motives, inclinations, dispositions, pursuits, habits and ways of thinking. But Millar is also saying that in making sense of such differences, and explaining how they come about, we can only proceed on the assumption that human beings, in all their particularity, remain social beings of an essentially similar sort. Only thus can we anticipate that, given a key difference in situation, there will be parallel differences in rules, behaviour and inclinations.

In sum

Sociology has inherited from the Enlightenment tradition a vital set of philosophical, political and ethical concerns, generating a series of tensions that remain highly productive for social science thinking. Sometimes these tensions – between sameness and difference, between relativism and universalism – seem almost impossible to resolve. Yet the general idea of sociological understanding as exemplified by Millar's statement has travelled remarkably well across the cultures and the centuries, in spite of the undoubtedly white, male, middle-class and Eurocentric proclivities of Millar and others like him.

Interchange

Question:

Are you supporting Millar just because you're Scottish?

Response:

Yes and No. 'Yes', because, as the question implies, all our intellectual preferences are shaped to some extent by our background identities and standpoints (= relativism). But also 'No', because as Millar's statement requires, we can still strive to attain a viable degree of detachment or generality in our understanding (= universalism). It is useful here to bear in mind the paradox that lies at the core of relativism: if the validity of all claims is strictly relative to particular social situations and subjective viewpoints, then none can be universally true. But this is itself a universal claim; therefore, it is both true and false; therefore, it is false.

4

Three founders

The prominence of the Scots is often said to have a sociological rationale: during the eighteenth century, the Highlands began to be cleared of its settled crofters to make way for commercial stock farming. Scientific modes of agriculture were introduced, and the towns of Scotland's central belt were becoming thriving centres of manufacture, finance and international trade in the burgeoning British Empire. This situation of rapid growth made particularly visible to historians and social thinkers the differences between the remnants of feudal and even tribal community that could still be observed in Scotland, and the thrusting mercantile-capitalist culture that was in the ascendancy.

In this context, people like Adam Ferguson and Adam Smith put forward an overarching theory of history in which there are four main stages of social change. The first is the hunter-gatherer stage, which is followed by pastoral (shepherd) society, which leads to settled and large agricultural civilizations, and finally the (to them) modern world of commerce and manufacture. This succession of phases was regarded as, on the whole, beneficial and necessary, and its logic was theorized as driven by improvements in the basic 'mode of subsistence' – the ways that food, shelter and clothing were produced and consumed. By comparison with previous understandings of history based on the alleged primacy of great ideas and great men, this was an innovative *materialist* sociological account, of the sort that Karl Marx would take further a century later.

The Scottish school affirmed that there had to be a necessary element of inevitable progress that led human society from a state of relatively simple and 'primitive' existence to 'advanced' or 'polished' commercial civilization. At the same time, they accepted that such progress had significant costs and gave rise to the possibility of a widening gulf between rich and poor – between rich and poor nations, too. Sociology thus came to life as a debate about the good and bad consequences of the three revolutions (Industrial, French, Enlightenment), and about how universal and inevitable was Western-style social development. With the further move from merchant-commercial society into industrial society, the contrasts between the traditional and modern eras became even more accentuated. Three names are particularly significant in this transition.

Saint-Simon

Henri Saint-Simon (1760–1825) was notable as a provocative enthusiast of industrialism, seeing it as a radically different type of civilization that promised a new kind of heroism. This French theorist continually drew analogies from the natural sciences to set social thinking on a sounder basis. He talked about 'social physics' and the 'solid' and 'fluid' properties of social life, and speculated that all social phenomena were governed by 'laws of attraction' in parallel to the Newtonian laws of gravity.

These ideas were then adjusted into the slightly different terminology of social physiology, in which societies were viewed as specific kinds of organism, exhibiting distinct principles of organization. Saint-Simon was a declamatory thinker, his chaotic thought aligning well with his life as a whimsical adventurer and unstable personality. More a prophetic voice than a careful theorist, there is nonetheless something original and exciting about Saint-Simon's passion to introduce a technocratic vocabulary that would do justice to the machine age and would herald the socially engineered future. Favoured ideas such as organization, planning and expertise gave Saint-Simon's outlook a logistical or technical connotation, as if procedures and precision are just as important as any substantive social or ethical end-result. Agitated by the disorder of the French revolutionary period – in which he suffered physically and mentally – Saint-Simon wanted the world to be redesigned, driven by the scientific mindset and piloted by the emerging professional elite of the industrial epoch. A prerequisite for this was to conceive society itself as having a stand-alone organizational logic, operating above the level of individuals with a spirit or consciousness of its own, and entirely autonomous from the clutches of the state.

In terms of ethics and politics, the future of humanity rested on the shoulders of the new productive classes – the bold entrepreneurs, the rational administrators, the scientific experts, the prototype designers and the skilled workers who were the force behind manufacturing. There was no place in this world for the parasitic landed classes and their 'weak' values and character (Saint-Simon himself was an aristocrat by background). In this vision, existing forms of property ownership are rejected, and increasingly harmonious endeavour among the new productive classes was expected to produce its own form of religion, rather misleadingly announced as the New Christianity. With this sort of spiritual collectivism in play, Saint-Simon is sometimes taken to be a forerunner of socialism. However, he lacked the commitment to popular democracy characteristic of socialist thinkers: in his society, an elite drawn from the productive classes would plan and rule on behalf of society as a whole, and the general masses would need to follow compliantly.

Comte

Auguste Comte (1798–1857) worked with Saint-Simon for a while, and the two shared many of the same ideas and ideals. They were both 'progressivists' and 'positivists'. Positivism in the social sciences means three main things, each of which can be taken in a strict, dogmatic way, or more flexibly. First, human social behaviour, though messy, is governed by underlying general laws of a certain kind. Second, sociology is a proper science; it may well have a distinctive subject-matter of its own, but in its investigative goals and methodology, it conforms to the protocols of other established sciences.

Third, positivism is normatively (i.e. morally and politically) committed to the cultural primacy of the scientific outlook, believing the latter to be pivotal in achieving true social progress.

In line with those positivist headlines, Comte saw the modern society that was forming in the wake of the French Revolution as irrational and chaotic, urgently in need of new solidarities and better theoretical anchors. Since intellectual order was a prerequisite for any stable social order, Comte's starting point was to draw attention to the developmental logic of scientific understanding itself. He espoused a three-phase account of the way that each genuine branch of knowledge individually evolves, and took this schema to be central to the progress of the collective Mind as a whole. (We might note here that Comte adopted an idealist view of the stages of human development, by comparison with the Scots' more materialist outlook.)

In the first, 'theological' stage, the causes of phenomena and the reasons why things exist as they do are attributed to the existence, motives and interventions of superior supernatural forces. (The theological stage, by the way, was also seen as having three stages nested within it – fetishism, polytheism, monotheism.)

Then comes the 'metaphysical' stage, in which our cognitive efforts are orientated not to the influence of personalized non-human beings, but rather to the abstract essences that give all things their core identity. In the metaphysical frame, we speculate that all things, and all types of similar things, possess an intrinsic nature, and we give these general names that we can appeal to for justification – 'nature', for example, or 'human nature', or 'justice', 'freedom', 'destiny' and the like.

Finally, there is the 'positive' stage, in which proper knowledge based on scientific theory and empirical observation comes to the fore. In this stage, we actively resist the temptation to turn to vacuous theological or metaphysical generalities, especially just for psychological and moral reassurance. Positive knowledge involves fearlessly rational comprehension, breaking things down into their specific ways of working, and generating solutions to problems by identifying the appropriate level at which they are caused and manifested. And for Comte, the solution to modernity's problems is not only to promote fully positive knowledge within the sciences, but to infuse politics with the same rational scientific spirit, thus producing a 'positive polity'.

Comte's theory of the three stages has frequently been regarded as absurdly simplistic and deterministic, but this is contestable. For one thing, Comte referred to 'states' not 'stages', and this word-change makes a difference, since it disturbs any assumption that all the 'stages' (= states) are of equal standing. For example, Comte regards the metaphysical state as being a zone of lesser integrity than the other two, being the site of battles between them and tending to slide more towards theological than to positive consciousness. This conception in turn works against any strict sense of inevitability in the idea of a prescribed passage through the sequence. It is also uncertain whether the succession of states was intended by Comte to apply to the development of society as such. It's certainly meant to characterize how each genuine branch of science gets finally established, and it's a good way of thinking about the contradictions and anxieties that grip our own personal development (Comte applied it to the ups and downs of his own turbulent anxieties). But it is less clear that the scheme applies precisely to world history as such, not least because the positive polity could still be some time coming. Comte thought that contemporary modernity was a mixed-up, metaphysical phase of society, and he saw the need for not only science, but imagination, fiction and moral example in dragging it forward towards the fully positive society.

Comte's second main contribution, related to the first, was to think of science in terms of a developing spectrum or hierarchy, not a single established model common to all disciplines. Each of the five main scientific fields that he discusses in his massive *Course in Positive Philosophy* – mathematics, astronomy, physics, chemistry and biology – had made their passage through the three states, but at different times and according to their different levels of generality. Thus, mathematics, the most general and abstract science, gets to the positive stage first, followed by astronomy, then physics and chemistry, and only very recently biology. Comte's point was that it is the progression through the three-states process itself, and not conformity to the very same types of laws or investigative methods, that makes a discipline scientific; also, some sciences can't achieve their full status until others have.

This actually makes Comte's positivism quite sophisticated. Biology is a science just like physics, but it is not the same sort of science as physics, and it is no less a science than physics, just because it needed physics to evolve first. Similarly, sociology – Comte coined the very term – should not be too concerned about being a hard science exactly in the manner of physics, because the regularities to be found in its objects of study are not the same sort of regularities as those in the higher sciences. Indeed, Comte inverted this idea of what was 'higher' and what was 'lower': biology, since it incorporates within itself the more general laws of physics and chemistry, and then adds furthers life principles of its own, should be seen as nearer the top of the hierarchy. By that same logic, Comte insisted, sociology stands not only as the sixth science, but is the very queen of the sciences.

But what is it that sociological science actually says and does, exactly? Other than being the one who repeatedly explains to scientists and others the law of the three states, and explains what sort of things that law applies to, the sociologist tries to identify the crucial rising factors that are present within a social situation and also, correspondingly, the factors that might be declining in evolutionary terms. This is achieved by comparative historical analysis and by projecting forward to possible positive futures.

Such advice was largely methodological; Comte seemed to run out of steam when it came to making lasting concrete sociological suggestions. He did argue that some parts of the metaphysical present (industry and science) were tending towards positivity, whilst others (morality, religion, politics) were retrograde. He also distinguished between social 'unions' (the family) that necessarily restricted creative specialization, and more fluid social 'associations' that stemmed from a more spontaneous division of labour in the wider economy. But these propositions were not very fertile, empirically. As for his political views, these were similar to Saint-Simon's, despite a phase in which Comte held out great hopes for the proletariat – the emerging industrial working class. Otherwise, to keep forward momentum, organizations and social decision-making would have to be hierarchical, requiring a technocratic vanguard and even a 'sociocracy' – rule by sociologists!

If there was always an element of the bizarre in Comte's thought, things got worse after the trauma experienced in his late forties when an intense (platonic) love affair ended with his partner's death just a year later. Comte then gave free reign to some of his wilder ideas about an elaborate, positivist Religion of Humanity. He turned his lover's memory into a kind of cult, seeking to revive ideas of chivalry and promoting the kind of inner purity that only women, he insisted, could exemplify.

Spencer

In common with Comte, Herbert Spencer (1820–1903) composed multi-volume treatises that knowledgeably placed sociology in the context of the other sciences of the day, especially biology. And Spencer, too, has seen something of a recovery of his reputation as someone who raised vital questions and made interesting contributions, rather than being just a relic languishing in the dusty history books. In political terms, Spencer was a consistent and unapologetic liberal of his day, which we would now identify with conservative or right-wing ideology. Virulently hostile to the idea of state interference, dismissive of the notion that society as a whole could develop a common consciousness and opposed to all attempts artificially to generate more social solidarity and altruism ('altruism' being another of Comte's inventions, incidentally), Spencer's produced his own famous signature phrase: survival of the fittest.

This arresting notion influenced Darwin, but Spencer delivered it as a moral punch-line as well as a scientific one. There was, he thought, nothing much to be done about the fit out-performing the weak in the course of human association, and in a sense it was nothing more than they deserved anyway. Because this sort of ultra-competitive ethos would be viewed as reprehensibly anti-social by most sociologists today, there have been quite serious obstacles to taking Spencer seriously. But even this aspect of Spencer reveals some underlying complications. For example, he seems to have felt that the advance that political reformers and revolutionaries could never achieve as a matter of exhortation would probably come of its own accord, in due course, through the evolutionary process itself. As people got used to exercising maximum individual freedom, for example, their selfishness would give way to broader expressions of advanced human life, taking up and reproducing concerns about the quality of society as a whole. So, Spencer was possibly not the misanthropic pessimist he is often made out to be.

Otherwise, there are three main Spencerian insights. As with Comte and several others, Spencer distinguished between 'social statics' and 'social dynamics', the first looking at what holds societies together in a coordinated whole, the second concentrating on sources of disruption and reintegration. In his own 'social statics', Spencer anatomized society according to a division between its regulating (political/military) sub-system, its sustaining (economic) sub-system and its distributing (social policy) sub-system. This is a useful way of conceptualizing social structure.

Next, Spencer offered a two-stage, rather than a three- or four-stage, model of social development. His two main categories were the 'militant' and the 'industrial' society. The first of these social types achieves coherence and purpose through coercion, based on elements in the social structure in which lines of hierarchy are clear, compulsory and generally accepted. The industrial model minimizes the need for direct force in human affairs, since the operation of the division of labour, markets for goods and contracts for services generate a spontaneous kind of social interdependence and order. The most obvious cases of militant forms of social organization arise when societies are actually at war, or when they seem to be on a kind of semi-permanent war-footing. Many tribal and feudal societies could feasibly be characterized in this way, for example. Now, given Spencer's approval of free-market capitalism, the projected evolution from the militant to the industrial appears to be a matter of straightforward progress for him. However, his distinction was not intended in such a crude way, because he made use of it to analyse the mixed tendencies within many societies. Fast-forwarding with Spencer in mind, we could use his categories and the various mixtures between them to understand political regimes like Margaret Thatcher's neo-liberal Britain in the 1980s ('free society, strong state'), or the Soviet bloc state socialist nations of 1945–89 ('command economies'). Similarly, the way in which the Western democracies responded to the plane attacks on New York in 2001 in terms of a coordinated 'war on terror' could be seen as the resumption of militant forms of organization and control in the midst of an otherwise industrial style of social organization.

The third part of Spencer's programme is his sense that all phenomena – from cosmic processes to biological organisms, or the social super-organism – develop through a pattern of aggregation, differentiation and coordination. That is to say, we start with some relatively simple, selfsame units that grow in number and combine to form a homogeneous mass. But this mass gradually becomes unmanageable and overloaded, so it splits up into differentiated variants, forming a more elaborate set of interdependencies. And as this new structural form then itself grows, it too requires reorganization as it reaches limits beyond which it cannot be sustained in the selfsame way. We therefore see cycles of dissolution/disintegration.

Spencer illustrated this general principle of growth, subdivision and reintegration in many social and historical ways, and it is instructive to try out some random examples of our own. We could use Spencer's concept to think about the growth, split and partial re-formation of, for example, sporting teams, friendship networks, professional organizations, the development of villages into towns, cities dividing into zones, firms into industrial sectors, political movements into forms of government, the formation and decline of social classes, and more. Spencer's point wasn't that social organization simply follows biological organization in all this, but that both sociology and biology provide their own kind of instances of the overarching sequence that encompasses all living forms. Spencer's thinking on all this has been strenuously criticized on many occasions, but today it once again looks rather more attractive. For example, it seems to tune in with the current widespread use of systems theory and complexity theory that many feel are not only scientifically productive in their own right, but also help significantly to bridge the gap between the natural sciences and social sciences.

Taking these three founders as a whole, we can summarize their intellectual deficits in terms of an obsessively scientistic (positivist) and unacceptably elitist quest for evolved order. Specifically, their style of thought has frequently been characterized and countered in the following way:

- Deterministic – as though the whole of social history has a goal and drive that is completely beyond the influence of active human beings, just as human biology and behaviour is 'all in the genes'.
- Organicist – but society and social groups are *not* organisms as such.
- Eurocentric – social evolutionism equates human progress with the self-justifying story that Western white men tell of themselves.
- Social Darwinist – notions of only the fittest surviving (and deserving to survive) have fuelled projects of social cleansing and eugenics.

Even if these critical points are broadly valid, they exaggerate the crudity of the founders' ideas and undervalue their theoretical interest. Moreover, sociologists today need to be careful not to lay down an equally dogmatic law that, because of the risk of social Darwinism, sociologists should never indulge in 'biologistic' thinking or never align themselves with evolutionary ideas coming from the natural sciences. The set of issues raised by these founders about the relationship between social and biological processes, and between biology and sociology, remains vital today. In any case, neither Darwin himself nor most modern biologists take ideas such as natural selection or descent with modification or reproductive fitness to refer to *inevitable* sequences of natural history, nor do they imply any sort of morally superior end-point. On the contrary, all evolutionary transitions and mechanisms are a matter of contingency (happenstance), and the question of which biological processes are strongly conditioned by social factors, and which less so, is an ongoing matter about which sociologists need to be scientifically knowledgeable to make their own points count.

In sum

Before and during the period of the Enlightenment, many philosophers and historians produced telling sociological concepts and insights. But in the nineteenth century sociology started to come into its own as a distinct form of study. The authors featured in this chapter explicitly adopted the term 'sociology', and felt that sociology was not just a way of thinking, but had a pivotal socio-political role to play in / modern society. This does not mean that we have to revere these 'founders': the social Darwinism that they espoused is fraught with dangers and problems. On the other hand, Saint-Simon, Comte and Spencer have often been unfairly downgraded, and the central questions they raised about the different ways of categorizing societies, and the relationship between social sciences and the life sciences, remain on the agenda today.

Interchange

Question:

They all sounded crazy, Comte and Saint-Simon anyway. What does this say about sociology?

Response:

As it happens, Spencer also had numerous bouts of paralysing anxiety and neurosis, and like Comte also decided that his ideas were better developed in complete isolation, paying no attention to what anyone else was thinking. Subsequent classic sociologists (notably Weber and Gilman, who we will meet soon) also suffered profound episodes of distress and collapse. Maybe the whole idea that drives much social theory in 'totalizer' mode is a bit mad, namely that you can build a relatively small set of concepts in your head that captures the very essence of the whole world, despite its manifestly vast scale and complexity. Today, such a demanding task is generally accepted as requiring a more collective, partial and ongoing approach.

5

Three classics

What counts as a 'classic' in an academic discipline is not a straightforward matter. It would not be very sociological to think that there was a permanent league table of great individual thinkers based solely on the brilliance or truth of their thoughts. Our estimates of classic-ness, therefore, cannot stand apart from traditional and current ideological and social concerns. Classic status might also depend on things like the availability and timing of translations from the original language in which the author wrote. Thus, of the authors summarized here, Max Weber (1864–1920) only entered the sociological canon (list of revered figures) in the 1940s, and Karl Marx (1818–83) in the 1960s, and the reasons given for such authors being regarded as classics are subject to continual scholarly dispute. This is why I refer to these figures, along with Emile Durkheim (1858–1917), as three classics rather than *the* three classics, as many textbooks did twenty years ago.

Certainly, if we compare Marx, Weber and Durkheim with those discussed in the last chapter, their ways of thinking about social development, about its costs and contradictions, and about sociological method appear to be more compelling. Civilization, Comte announced, has 'under every aspect, made constant progress', but this would be an impossible sentiment for the later trio. Additionally, the earlier writers were philosophical speculators in the main – though we must acknowledge that Spencer pioneered several volumes of empirical materials (collected by assistants) under the attractive title Descriptive Sociology. But Marx, Durkheim and Weber were perhaps more consistently absorbed in the task of grounding their big pictures of the social world in the painstaking study of data and patterns concerning such things as the state of public health, working conditions, suicide, corporate and economic growth, ancient and modern history, the variety of religions and more besides.

Let's compare the sociological big pictures of these three classics according to four aspects of social theorizing. (These also guided the discussion in the previous chapter, but only implicitly.)

1   Social change: the development of society, and especially modernity, over time.
2   Social structure: analysis of the most important social elements and relationships.
3   Philosophical preferences: a) 'epistemology' – how theorists justify their accounts by reference to ideas about proper knowledge/science, and b) 'ontology' – their assumptions concerning the nature of social existence.
4   Normative stance: their ideological and political inclinations and goals.

Marx

Marx envisaged the development of history as a sequence of societal types governed by their prevailing modes of production. This idea refers to how societies organize the production and reproduction of their material basis, and for Marx they are most specifically distinguished from one another by the ways in which economic surplus is generated and 'appropriated'. Marx argued that inequalities and conflicts between socio-economic classes had characterized all known human history and that these were, in turn, crucially connected to the fundamental social division that exists between the direct producers of economic outputs and the (minority) social stratum — the dominant or ruling class — that expropriates whatever surplus arises. Each of the modes of production is marked by a unique set of relations of production — the forms of wealth generation and associated legal and social institutions that define the (unequal) powers of ownership and entitlement of the principal classes. For example, Marx identified an ancient or slave mode of production in classical Greece and Rome, where the ruling class directly owned the means of production and the human labourers themselves, and where the large-scale, slave-based cultivation of the land was central to wealth production. He defined a feudal mode of production, in which the labour was also primarily land-based, but this time on a smaller scale, and in which the labourers were not directly owned as such by the landowning ruling class. Rather, peasants worked the fields for their own subsistence, in addition to which they delivered an obligatory extra amount (whether in kind, or in service, or in money) to the feudal lord.

Marx believed that history was essentially dynamic; it could not be held frozen according to the rules of any particular mode of production as long as that mode was based on profound class exploitation. Accordingly, he maintained that certain tendencies within each mode would steadily sharpen latent social contradictions and cause technological blockages. He also held that the levels and conscious awareness of class conflict would intensify, until the point came when a combination of such objective and subjective factors would result in a revolutionary breakthrough into an altogether different type of society/mode of production.

Applying this outlook – sometimes called historical materialism – to the Victorian Britain of his own day, Marx defined capitalism as the generalized production of all commodities for sale on the market, including, uniquely, labour power itself. That is to say, in a capitalist system, workers have to sell their talents and abilities on the open market to employers, who pay cash for the use of that labour power. We say 'labour power' here because what the capitalist is buying is the capacity of the labourer to produce a flexible range of output, not a given fixed quantity of work. And typically, according to Marx, the value of the product derived from labour contributed exceeds the cost of reproducing the labourers' capacity to work, so he calls this difference 'surplus value'.

Surplus value is the source of all profit in a capitalist economy, and it is the more scientific concept, because a) it refers more precisely to the actual source of money-making in capitalism, and b) it shows how capitalism, whatever the level of wages (which might be quite high at times), is an intrinsically exploitative system. Of course, Marx was well aware that the profit motive drove capitalist activity, but profit is a positively misleading term because it is too easily construed as the more or less fair 'reward' for the subjective effort or cleverness of individual capitalists. Similarly, even if wages appear to be the more or less fair result of a contract freely entered into by both worker and employer, it is not the actual labour that is paid for by the capitalist but rather the labour power, which means that even if capitalists are thought to be giving whatever they can reasonably afford in wages, they are all the time deriving surplus, and also retaining the ability to intensify or relax the conditions of labour according to circumstances. For Marx, the personal attributes of particular employers and workers are largely irrelevant in seeking to grasp how capitalism works as a system.

Given the profit motive and the logic of surplus value production, Marx traced how phases of capitalist competition amongst multiple rival firms in a sector would be followed, in an ever-intensifying spiral, by strong moves to monopoly as profits became squeezed and as available forms of technology reached the maximum level of labour intensification compatible with them. Bouts of restructuring would then take place, with those firms and cartels that could develop new forms of labour-saving technology taking the advantage and others falling by the wayside. In Marx's terminology, it is vital to note, machinery and techniques do not represent a stand-alone factor of production; they are nothing other than 'congealed' labour – the product of previous 'live' labour, now transferred to the subsequent labour process cycle.

If these things seem merely economic, Marx asks us to look more carefully. An entire socio-economic dynamic is unleashed, he thinks, whereby the intrinsic tendencies of the capitalist mode of production eventually generate social and political crisis. With the emergence of larger and larger conglomerate firms and their ever-higher dependence on labour-shedding technology comes a more massified and periodically under-employed working class. Partly because the technological and market aspects of capitalist society – so apparently impersonal – are merely the 'reified' (thingified) product of human labouring activity itself, there is a growing process of alienation of the mass of working humanity from the essentially dehumanizing spirit of capitalism. Glimmers of the idea that capitalism is fundamentally unjust develop, not only on account of its regime of economic exploitation, but because it holds back the truly creative, cooperative character of human labour. Yet, as it happens, capitalism itself has relentlessly rendered society more culturally and economically uniform; it has brought into view the enormous emancipatory power of science and technology; and it has caused the working class to be more concentrated in numbers and outlook. Developing over time a collectivist and progressivist consciousness, the proletariat reaches in its struggles towards a non-exploitative, non-alienated form of socio-economic existence. Thus, the subjective understanding of the exploited class would come to coincide with the escalating objective irrationalities of capitalist boom and bust, and a profound revolutionary change would occur, whether cataclysmic and violent or not (Marxists have argued about this ever since).

Marx, then, developed an explanatory theory – historical materialism – in relation to social change, and saw the social structure of current history not as modernity per se, but as capitalism above all. In politics and ideology he was a revolutionary socialist, aiming for an advanced form of communism, a democratically organized and scientifically knowledgeable society of ever-flourishing individuals.

As for Marx's philosophical outlook, this combines a 'dialectical materialist' ontology and a 'scientific realist' or critical realist epistemology. The first of these labels, dialectical materialism, indicates Marx's view that whilst the world as a whole is ultimately physical in character – he has no place for gods or other-worldly forces – it is also dynamic and multidimensional, social existence especially. Some previous materialist philosophers had conceived the 'matter' out of which the world is built as essentially separate, simple and static, but Marx saw it as interactive, moving and contradictory. He was consequently more interested in the nature of relationships, and above all, of course, social relationships, rather than the nature of brute things. Marx accepted that these contained a rich and important 'ideal' aspect, namely the world of thoughts, culture and beliefs. He called this the realm of 'ideology'. But he was not a philosophical idealist: the world of ideas and beliefs is derivative from, and ultimately to be explained by, the natural world of which human existence is a part, and from the social world in which material (socio-economic) interests predominate. Marx understood his dialectical materialist outlook to succeed the dialectical idealism of the German thinker he most admired, Hegel.

The more epistemological side of Marx's philosophy could be termed scientific realism, because he thought that the social and natural worlds were objective realities, and that his own studies were contributing to the growth of objective knowledge about the world. At the same time, the powers of abstraction that we have to use in our efforts to reveal the innermost secrets of the natural – and especially the socio-economic – world, are subject to ideological and political influences and motivations. And for Marx a true understanding of socio-economic life could only be achieved with commitment to progressive values and revolutionary rigour. Thus, he regularly polemicized against (pseudo-) scientific conceptions of economic exchange and abstract conceptions of political liberty that in his view amounted to bourgeois apologetics. The free market, for example, or equality before the law, taken as uncontextualized principles, amounted to ideological illusions, mistaking the surface appearances of capitalist society for the deeper reality.

So Marx was a scientific realist, but undoubtedly a critical one, including being critical of the positivist idea of a politics-free knowledge. Later realists have regarded this combination as the great merit of this philosophical stance, whilst other philosophers have felt that Marx's attempt to combine strong values with scientific objectivity was doomed to failure.

Durkheim

When it comes to Durkheim and Weber, we are dealing with the generation that established sociology as a university subject, produced the first sociological journals and set up the first national sociology associations. Western capitalist modernity and its nation-state system had bedded down, forming a societal world that was accepted by these thinkers as inescapable, legitimate (on the whole) and complex. If profound social inequalities undoubtedly existed, these did not stack up into just one sort of exploitation or one sort of power-wielding. Rather, modern societies were about numerous different layers of stratification and corresponding problems of social integration.

Of all the classics, Durkheim is the quintessential moderate (if undoubtedly a passionate moderate). He shared something of the social evolutionary outlook of Spencer and Comte, but he rejected the former's amoral approach to the logic of historical development, and the latter's idealist portrayal of its content (the three states theory of intellectual progression). He agreed with Marx that there were some things that were seriously wrong with capitalism, but he felt that these could be ameliorated by enlightened reform guided by sociological understanding (echoes here, but only faint ones, of Saint-Simon). Sociology, for its part, was affirmed as a properly scientific pursuit, autonomous from both philosophy and psychology. But the social facts that sociology distinctively studied, while statistically demonstrable, were not the same kind of thing as the facts of physics or biology. This was because they were significantly *moral* in character, meaning that sociologists had to be ethically as well as scientifically engaged. In particular, Durkheim felt that sociology could play both a diagnostic and a curative role in turning the 'pathological' elements of selfish, consumerist individualism in modernity into a more wholesome, humanistic vision of the socially minded individual.

For Durkheim, the key notion in understanding the logic of social change is not so much class struggle or capitalist development, as for Marx, but the idea of the division of labour as an index of progressive social differentiation. His starting point in this regard, and a familiar social evolutionist move, was to draw a strong contrast between traditional and modern societies. In traditional – or pre-modern, or tribal, or 'segmental' – societies, a very simple form of the division of labour exists, unambiguous and unquestioning, with any specialist roles (for example, to do with magic or healing) strongly constrained by the fixed norms of kin and clan group-life, themselves profoundly structured by the binding religious dictates of primitive society, all cemented in place by ritual practices dedicated to recognized deities and totems. Life and thought in traditional society was thus, according to Durkheim, essentially homogeneous; its component units are identical; people repeatedly do the same things; and they instinctively know their roles and places. This social division of labour is therefore characterized by what Durkheim termed 'mechanical solidarity'.

Such a rigid form of social organization presumes the perpetuation of a static social and natural environment. But, of course, this does not hold: primitive societies face serious survival challenges in times of material scarcity and ecological adversity, and when times are better, population grows, putting new demands on the capacity and culture of the core social units. In due course, the horde becomes the tribe, and tribes combine into tribal federations, which come into conflict with one another over resources and status. These types of evolutionary pressure eventually lead to more complex and dynamic divisions of labour, and correspondingly less totally binding social norms. In this typically modern situation (though it can be traced across several centuries), we are dealing with 'organic solidarity', in which people become simultaneously more individuated and yet also more interdependent. This process of social differentiation – ever-increasing specialization, individuation and large-scale interdependency – is for Durkheim the key structural feature of modernity. Most people find Durkheim's phraseology odd at first, because 'organic' seems to connote natural, while 'mechanical' suggests modern. However, we should think of mechanical as unthinkingly automatic and organic as signalling complex interdependency across the whole of the social system.

Durkheim's understanding of the key structures of the modernization process had a definite materialist side to it, as his interest in divisions of labour confirms. But what sets him apart from Marx is not only that he emphasized a different aspect of materiality, such that class divisions, though important, were not primary. Additionally, Durkheim grasped social structure as a matter of the different types of non-material social bonds and norms that prevail, the modes of fellow-feeling and the state of the collective consciousness. This emphasis in turn entails giving greater centrality to the social force of morality and religion than materialist sociologists are inclined to allow. For Durkheim, these expressions of social belonging and human interdependency are what we mean by the very idea of 'the social'.

Take Durkheim's studies of religion. At first, he advanced a relatively simplistic view of 'simple' societies, including their religious dimension. What tribal peoples were worshipping in their ritual and totemic practices was, Durkheim asserted, society itself. That is to say, religious practices provided a potent vehicle for concretizing the remarkable power of belonging to a collective reality of interactive, charged moral solidarity. It was the charge and the solidarity that counted, not the truth of the religious sentiments themselves. But in his later work, without ceasing to be a basically secular thinker, Durkheim shows greater appreciation of the symbolic complexity of ritual and totemism. He felt that these forms of the religious life not only reflect the reality of the social, they constitute it – they make it possible. This is because religious consciousness generates the sort of categories without which the social world cannot be either meaningful or coherently ordered. Such categories included the contrast between sacred and profane, normal and deviant, and good and evil. So even if religion is ultimately about the power of the social rather than the power of supernatural influences, it is the special sort of 'collective effervescence' that religion or religious-like commitments bring that heightens people's awareness of collective existence, and motivates them to celebrate it.

The moral categorization that articulates social being carries on into secular modernity, too, though in a weaker form. The law, for example, only has legitimacy because of our sentiment that, ultimately, the law upholds the value and deservingness of good citizens, not bad ones. Durkheim, we might note, felt that a certain amount of crime and deviance was to be accepted as normal and necessary, because it had the continual effect of reinforcing general social standards and triggered thoughts of who best exemplifies them. Moreover, most people in modernity, Durkheim supposes, hold that the main point of penal sanctions is to reform people into becoming better members of the community, not to indulge in physical retribution for its own sake. (He referred to this as the contrast between 'restitutive' and 'repressive' law.)

Sociologists in the later twentieth century revived these Durkheimian themes by noting how even eminently civic things to do with the nation and public institutions took on a kind of 'sacred' character – loyalty to the flag, coronations of monarchs, football world cups, war memorials and so on. Similarly, Durkheimian explanations were provided following the surprisingly widespread outpourings of grief in Britain following the death of Diana, Princess of Wales, in 1997. These collective emotions were considered to be effervescent expressions of social identification and profound, inexplicable sadness in the face of a lost symbolic community.

In terms of his philosophical outlook, Durkheim has often been described as a positivist, though the exact meaning of this term is much debated in the social sciences, as already noted. Certainly, he thought that sociology was a science and that society was a kind of organism, developing according to a certain logic and analysable in terms of its balance or imbalance between normal healthy phenomena and pathological ones. In his renowned 'rules of sociological method' he advocated treating social facts as things – objective, obdurate existences that we experience as forces and constraints coming from outside ourselves, rather than freely chosen. These social realities, even though essentially symbolic and moral, can be carefully observed, measured and causally explained. The sign of social facthood, Durkheim thought, was the way in which norms and values impinged upon us as if they were necessities, and the way in which they carry definite social sanctions of one kind or another that we implicitly recognize in our feelings and conduct. Thus, for example, in most societies there are prohibitions on incest, lying, cheating, adultery, murder, betrayal and so forth that are implicitly understood by all even if they are breached occasionally. And in modernity there are social facts produced by institutions that, whilst not perhaps directly moral as such, are still normative, serving to enforce cooperative and solidaristic behaviour. Examples here might be the rules (whether explicit or tacit) of driving on the appropriate side of the road, queuing up to buy tickets, taking on board the expectations of what it is to be a good worker, soldier or academic, and so on.

Sociology's task was thus to analyse and generalize about social facts, to dig into their causal rationale and to help counteract observed pathological tendencies. Durkheim was particularly concerned about the growth, in modernity, of 'anomie' – a state of growing normlessness, or individually experienced moral disorientation, in the face of a world that was losing its automatic reference points for action and behaviour, and its sense of intimacy. He argued that there was a specific type of 'anomic' suicide related to these specifically modern experiences, distinguishing it from other types ('egoistic', 'altruistic' and 'fatalistic' suicide). While psychology, no doubt, could tell us something about the personal motivation of people when they took their own lives, it was sociology's task to unearth the deeper social reasons for such actions when taken by significant numbers of people, as the statistics showed (or so he believed).

Durkheim's political and ideological views have been described as liberal reformist or, when interpreted more radically, as social-democratic. He was certainly a supporter of the French Third Republic, believing in benign nationalism and in the possibility of a third way between the two dangers of advanced modernity, namely rampant asocial individualism on the one hand and revolutionary socialist collectivism on the other. Durkheim thought that the decline of the craft guilds of early modernity had eroded the crucial levels of social solidarity that lay between the modern state and the individual, and he sought to revive this level of moral and personal identification by emphasizing the positive role that professional life and professional associations could play, both within the workplaces and in civic culture more generally.

Weber

Max Weber is probably the most hard-headed and multidimensional of the major sociological thinkers, and the one who undertook the broadest range of scholarly studies, covering legal systems, ancient civilizations, religions, agricultural labour conditions, economic practices, and art and music. For those reasons, Weber is often rated the best sociologist of all. This is slightly paradoxical, though, because Weber's work was very interdisciplinary, and he was sceptical about whether the sort of collective phenomena that sociologists like to summon up – like Marx's class, or Durkheim's collective consciousness, or even 'society' itself – refer to objectively existing realities. He accepted that we can devise interesting names for various large-scale social features and trends, but they don't actually refer to anything over and above innumerable singular events and the innumerable thoughts and actions of individuals. This view is sometimes termed 'methodological individualism', which most sociologists tend to think runs directly against their basic outlook.

In getting to grips with social change and the coming of modernity, Weber avoided any grand-stage theory of history. Different epochs and types of society came and went, certainly, but they did not pass into one another as if part of an inevitable sequence, and certainly not a sequence that showed that the world was bound to get progressively better. Weber consciously lacked Marx's heroic sense that a great flourishing of humanity was possible and necessary once the iniquities of class society were overcome, and he lacked Durkheim's modest optimism about the prospects of 'good' individualism and solidaristic reform.

Weber nevertheless shared the concern of the others to explain the emergence of capitalist modernity and to reflect on its ethical consequences. For Weber, although modernity was not necessarily a good thing, and although there was nothing morally superior about the West as such, he argued that it was only in Europe that a series of factors came together to make modern capitalism possible as a social type, soon to become the dominant one across the globe. He contrasted European modernity with ancient and medieval China, for example, holding that the latter's paternalistic, bureaucratic culture amongst the elites and the settled village clan communities, in which the mass of the peasantry lived, stifled the intellectual dynamism, individual entrepreneurship and social mobility that capitalism required. In the West, however, power was much more spread out across different power sources (monarchs, regional aristocrats, independent city authorities, merchant groups, craft guilds and the like) than in the East, and a decisive additional factor was the emergence of stringent, ascetic varieties of Protestant Christianity.

In worldviews such as Calvinism, the individual stood in direct relation to God, not mediated by complex, corrupt layers of clerics and rituals, as in pre-Reformation Catholic times. This was a humbling and terrifying existential situation, Weber suggested, not least in terms of how to handle the question of personal salvation. If, as was believed, the Protestant God had already set the world on a predestined course, then nothing we could do would alter His decision on who was to be elected for eternal life in heaven and who wasn't. Yet, perhaps signs of God's will on this might be glimpsed, with surely the possibility at least that the people who would be elected were those who worked hard and piously, dedicated themselves to good works in the world, behaved conscientiously and selflessly, deferred any personal gratification and generally disapproved of sensuous pleasure. Weber's famous 'Protestant Ethic thesis', then, was that, by happy coincidence, these beliefs about our fate in the next world were hugely conducive to 'capitalist' habits in the present world – production not consumption, saving not wasting, networking amongst trusted others and spreading a spirit of trust, duty and attention to detail in everything we do, including manufacture and trade. Our spiritual calling to do God's will thus turned out to be a calling to the spirit of capitalism, giving rise to considerable upward mobility and the accumulation of wealth for further capitalistic investment and growth.

If, to get going, capitalism needed this initial injection of spirituality from outside, so to speak, the bitter irony for the faithful was that in its developed form, modernity came to have no need whatsoever of Protestantism as such, nor any particular religion. Instead, the logic of capitalism becomes completely impersonal and essentially secular. Indeed, capitalist modernity actively sucks out of our institutions and interactions any sense of spirituality, magic, the irrational, the charismatic and the supernatural. The world becomes steadily more 'disenchanted' as the process of 'rationalization' takes hold. Everything, and everyone, become subject to rules and expectations that are calculable, standardized, predictable and instrumental. We are coming to live, Weber gloomily concluded, in an 'iron cage' of bureaucratic rationality, a totally administered society.

In that Weberian scenario of explaining modern social change, particular emphasis was placed on the importance of one belief system. But while Weber deliberately put this forward as a provocative alternative to the typical Marxist focus on socio-economic factors alone, Weber's point was not to say that material factors are unimportant, or that ideas were all-important. Rather, his approach to analysing social structure is multi-factorial — there are always a number of relevant factors to consider. In addition to socio-economic and ideational factors, considerations of power and domination were also vital for Weber. Again, he accepted that these are closely interrelated with economic and ideological elements: in the latter case, this is because forms of power and domination are especially effective when they coincide with legitimate authority. In all walks of life, those whose authority is considered legitimate tend to be held in esteem; they have status, which is another social factor in its own right. So each of the societal dimensions — economic, ideological, political — has its own rationale. Political behaviour is set apart because of the way in which parties — which does not mean just political parties, but any interested party in a power struggle of some kind — mobilize their support and how they conduct various practices of 'social closure', creating groups of 'insiders' who are distributed rewards for their efforts. For example, even if workers are dominated by capitalists (Weber did not deny this), it's still the case that men in the workplace can exercise power over women workers, and white workers can discriminate against black workers. In those scenarios, there are conflicts and practices of domination through social closure that cut across other conflicts and are not reducible to material advantages.

Weber's philosophical views about sociological method have three main planks. The first is that good social science must always pay close attention to the actual understandings and motivations experienced by real individuals. Thus, our interpretations of what is going on must be, in Weber's phrase, adequate at the level of meaning as well as at the level of the abstract, long-term causality. In other words, we need to be trying to get inside the heads and hearts of those we study. This is why sociology is as much about empathetic understanding as it is about scientific generalization.

That said, sociology *does* also have to generalize; we have to create encompassing categories and think about general social causes by grouping experiences together in a certain way. Here comes Weber's second methodological contribution. He points out that all our collective terms are intellectual constructions, not brute realities as such. But it is not as if we can avoid engaging in constructing general concepts, because we simply cannot make sense of the teeming, streaming data of experience unless we cut it up in some way. We do this, Weber says, through the use of 'ideal types', concepts that deliberately accentuate a particular way of looking at things, and that can be placed in a spectrum of one kind or another. For example, capitalism and feudalism are ideal types, referring to whole phases of social systems. But ideal types can apply to any level of social action. For instance, Weber typologized social action according to the different forms of rationality that they exhibit – 'traditional', 'affectual', 'instrumental' and 'value' rationality. And these in turn were related to what Weber held to be different kinds of legitimate authority ('traditional', 'charismatic' and 'legal-rational').

To approve the use of ideal types in these ways, but also to exercise caution about assuming that they map on to reality directly, is known as 'neo-Kantian' epistemology. The great German Enlightenment philosopher Immanuel Kant certainly did not doubt that reality in itself exists, but we can never know its ultimate real nature. We can only proceed by understanding the (physical) world through the lens of the categories that came already built-in to our apparatus of cognition, such as cause-and-effect and space-and-time. Weber and other neo-Kantians transferred this idea to the social and cultural spheres, which even more than nature had to be evaluated according to the application of deliberately one-sided ideal types. The social world was simply too vast and complex for us to know what it is like in itself, so we read it through the production and testing of ideal types, which always remain artificial, however interesting and appealing they may be.

The third plank of Weber's epistemology concerned the relation of science to values, and the way that he split the difference between an objectivist view and a subjectivist view of these issues. On the one hand, all the work we undertake as sociologists is 'value relevant' – we pick our topics of study because we find them valuable and morally relevant, and this can never be a purely objective matter. What matters is what matters to us. On the other hand, it is our duty as social scientists – Weber even brings up the term 'calling' again – it is our calling, our vocation, to try to proceed in a 'value-neutral' way. None of us, after all, likes it when people say that what we are presenting as fact simply reflects our personal ideological prejudices. We do have values, but we hope that we can demonstrate that they are not just our values, and therefore in various ways seek to be value neutral.

What about Weber's own ideological positions? He strongly felt that, because socialism (whatever the intention) would result in a world that was even more bureaucratized and disenchanted than liberal capitalism, one had little alternative but to be a liberal. But Weber was a pessimistic liberal because he saw little chance of the door of the iron cage of rationality flying open and some more deeply creative form of life taking over. Perhaps a strong blast of German nationalism would re-enchant modernity? Perhaps we could look forward to some kind of new charismatic leader who would take us something more thrilling, socially speaking? Weber leant in both these directions (and you can probably glean here that he had little faith in democracy). In the end, though, Weber's politics were ethical rather than political, strictly speaking, which is partly what we mean by someone being a liberal. At bottom, Weber thought, it was only as individuals, embedded in a depressingly conformist society, that we had to undergo the ordeal of deciding what we stand for, both morally and intellectually. Thus, for Weber, commitment is nothing less than an ordeal, because in a world of many aspects and many values, properly weighing all things up is truly difficult. There are always alternative, but equally partial, views we could take up. But decide we must, and when we do, we must take ethical responsibility for the choices we make.

In sum

Marx: a revolutionary socialist whose historical materialist concepts of capitalism and class were developed along 'critical realist' philosophical lines.

Durkheim: a republican reformist liberal whose neo-positivist rules of sociological method generated influential ideas of solidarity and anomie, division of labour and collective effervescence.

Weber: a pessimistic 'ethical' liberal, whose multidimensional studies of culture, economy and power were framed within a neo-Kantian epistemology of value-relevant ideal types.

Interchange

Question:

More large mouthfuls that presumably we will need to chew over and make some notes on. Meanwhile, are these 'classics' really still relevant to our situation today?

Response:

Definitely. Marx's vision of proletarian revolution has always seemed too extreme for liberals, but most socialists also increasingly regard it as unfeasible. His claims for the centrality of socio-economic class, too, are routinely criticized. But there are huge inequalities between rich and poor people today, and they are growing not lessening. There are rust belts and sink estates and vast swathes of semi-menial jobs that have something to do with the class position that people fall into when they put their labour-power on to the market and face the results. As for the supposition that the majority of people today in liberal capitalist societies, being middle-class, are doing OK, it needs to be noted that Marx never said the working class had to be manual workers toiling in factories, only that they were the sort who could not survive without selling their labour. This applies to a great many people in the 'middle', who seem to survive on debt and mortgages rather than piles of cash. And many professionals – university lecturers for example – are having to fight for their jobs, experience a decline in status and pay, and see their levels of autonomy at work erode.

More generally, Marx's core argument about capitalism, namely that its intrinsic volatility and irrationality leads to the steady globalization, centralization and concentration of wealth, and that this in turn causes the rich to get richer while the poor get poorer (relatively at least), seems to many people to have been vindicated by the serious world financial crisis that broke out in 2007–8, and that continues to rumble on in 2010.

American sociologist George Ritzer coined the neat phrase 'McDonaldization of Society' to characterize contemporary work and life. But Ritzer freely acknowledges that all he is really doing is updating Weber's idea of rationalization. Where Weber himself highlighted the bureaucratic aspect of organizations, Ritzer switches focus to the fast-food industry. But the same ingredients, so to speak, are present: the constant drive towards efficiency achieved through fixed rules and behaviour monitored for consistency; increasingly precise calculation and methods of gauging efficiency (time spent on different operations, costs per unit of output/consumption); and greater predictability of both process and product. And once this model succeeds in one sphere of instrumental rationality, it spreads to others – not only tyre-fitting centres and DIY stores, but also health service provision, university degrees and endless, mindless regulations seeking to secure the 'safety' of the citizen. The rather grim disenchantment of the world that is going on here is only confirmed by commercially driven injections of everyday 'charisma' in the form of 'Have a Nice Day' salutations and the smiling countenance of Ronald McDonald.

As for Durkheim, we have already seen that his notion of collective effervescence can still apply to contemporary civic rituals and collective symbolic identifications. His concern about pathological or anomic (normless) experiences travels well, too, and numerous phenomena can be usefully approached in these terms: tendencies towards consumerism and obesity, widespread everyday 'rage', youthful binge-drinking and alienated behaviour in school, our seeming inability or unwillingness to hold monogamous relationships together, parental obsession about the safety and achievement of their children, and so on. Of course, many religious people regard this condition of Durkheimian anomie as the direct consequence of secularization, the recipe for which is a strong revival of faith. But you don't have to be religious to wish for more 'sacred' forms of meaning, spirituality and togetherness (solidarity) in an increasingly differentiated society.

6

Three other classics

In Europe, the ideas of progress and enlightenment lost their gleam after the dreadful carnage of the First World War (1914–18). There was greater awareness of societal complexity, and of the moral and intellectual difficulties of all one-dimensional theses, whether in science or politics. As it became established as a subject in universities, sociology gave more attention to the subtle details of culture and consciousness, whilst remaining highly responsive to the maelstrom of history sweeping around it. The global impact of the Bolshevik Revolution ensured that Marxist ideas were never far from the centre of discussion, whether in Europe or in the United States, where sociology started to boom in the 1890s and where 'progressivism' remained quite strong after it faded in Europe. Particularly notable was the way in which, due to the rise of feminist and African-American thought, basic conceptions of social change and social structure were both challenged and also extended.

Simmel

The fairly sharp dividing lines between objectivity and subjectivity, and between sensuous, emotional life and the more structural 'macro' issues favoured by Marx and Durkheim, became creatively blurred in the work of Georg Simmel (1858–1918). Denied a significant academic post in his native Germany at least partly because he was Jewish, and more aware of the challenges posed to sociology by the changing status of women than many of his male peers, Simmel played up the growing discrepancy, within modernity, of objective impersonal trends and systems on the one hand, and the world of subjective life on the other. Simmel did not lack understanding of the larger structures of society – he wrote a treatise on the role of money within capitalism, for example, and he noted the overall trends in social consumption that led to mass interest in fashion. But he was critical when large-scale sociology seemed to turn into generalized philosophies of history, insisting that the 'tissues' and small-scale connections that ran between the main 'organs' of society were just as important as the latter. Accordingly, he gave more attention to sociological description, and to the cultural, the sensuous and purely sociable aspects of interaction than the other big names of his time.

Simmel developed what has been called the method of 'formal sociology' to try to grasp the relations between objective and subjective, and between sameness and difference. By a social form he meant any relation between people that could be specified over and above the particular sites and contents of that relation. Domination, for instance, could apply to the relation between lords and peasants, men and women, and teachers and students. Other key large-scale social forms might be exchange or cooperation. These formal concepts tell us what kind of situation a given episode of interaction is, and bring out some intriguing and important parallels across differences. For example, wars between nations and marital breakdowns alike can be thought to be cases of interactive social conflict. Thus, we might observe across the two otherwise different settings: a steady increase in tension that is not relieved by official (usually unsuccessful) efforts to communicate; stand-off periods when neither partner accepts the blame for apparently rather minor problems or events; the eruption of explicit antagonism when both parties have to concentrate on winning even if it means behaving badly or lying; and the emergence of a publicly recognized settlement (a treaty, a divorce certificate).

In latching on to the inner logistics and psychology of situations, Simmel flagged up the importance of sheer numbers for how people think, strategize and behave in relation to their social partners. He noted for example how the special nature of obligation and trust in two-person relationships – 'dyads' – alters definitively when third parties come on the scene to form interactive 'triads'. Similarly, the basic feelings and behaviours associated with triads shift again when the principle unit of a situation is the small group. And when groups become crowds, again, major sociological changes occur alongside changes in scale and density. As well as numbers, Simmel produced many insights into the workings of social types and roles, which are also forms in his sense. These would include major functional categories like boss, worker, bureaucrat and wife (Simmel was more alive than other male classics to questions of gender and their centrality to cultural understanding). But in addition, Simmel highlighted less obvious, but still typical, styles of conduct. He discussed what happens to a group when a stranger comes in from outside, something that tends to have a mixture of beneficial and adverse consequences. He was also struck by the mindset, and the impact on others, of types like gamblers, hustlers and lovers.

Simmel's way of understanding such roles can be described as 'phenomenological' because this latter term refers to the way we experience the inner and outer worlds, including such basic coordinates as space and time. The committed gambler, for instance, might regard the elapse of long periods of time during an ordinary day as little more than a lost opportunity for laying bets, and might come even to perceive each passing person or event through the lens of a wager. ('I bet she's going to meet her muscle-bound boyfriend in the Thekla club'; 'Three to one he's just stolen that bike'.)

Simmel was particularly acute on the phenomenology associated with living in the new metropolis of the twentieth century. In the modern city, things come to seem less permanent, more fleeting and more superficial compared with non-urban settings in the past, and we quickly adjust to this and almost savour the results. Thus, Simmel describes the vast array of sensations involved even in such an ordinary action as crossing a busy street (crowds, traffic, quickened pace, noises, neon lights, 'buzz'). And he showed the sociological-moral relevance of the ever more rapid cycle of sense-stimulation and subsequent sense-dulling. Thus, in the perpetual throng, bustle and diversity of social conditions and social types in the modern city, what one moment is the source of great liveliness and attentiveness in us, the next moment becomes a source of spiritual and moral indifference, as we become habituated to it. Simmel called this syndrome the metropolitan 'blasé', the way in which we become rather aloof and unheeding of the real problems of others. We might even develop a certain aloof style as a distinguishing mark (think 'cool').

Gilman

Women of the Victorian era in Britain made notable contributions to politics and sociology. Harriet Martineau (1802–76), for example, translated Comte into English and produced many comparative reports on social life in diverse cultural settings; Florence Nightingale (1820–1910) grounded her passionate commitment to nursing reform in her pioneering statistical depictions of health practices; and Beatrice Potter Webb (1858–1943) researched with precision and insight into the London poor, working conditions, industrial democracy and the cooperative movement. In the United States, the work of Charlotte Perkins Gilman (1860–1935) was especially searching, both theoretically and subjectively, helping to establish gender relations and women's subordination as core sociological concerns.

Influenced by Spencer and others, Gilman explicitly identified with sociology as a label, regarding it as a truly vital project, both scientifically and morally. Humanity, she thought, stood on the threshold of a truly higher level of civilization, characterized by the collectivization of major societal tasks, governed by intelligent coordination and expanding enormously our interdependent capacity for action. Within this evolved mutuality, we would live happy and fulfilled lives. For Gilman, sociology itself was the appropriate mindset for such social advance, together with thoroughgoing socialization in the virtues and advantages of societal coordination. In her utopian novel *Herland* – Gilman wrote much fiction and poetry – out of the three men imagined as encountering a women-only island society, it is only the sociologist that learns from it in the right way, and who then contributes some astute comments about the mixed effects of doing without males.

But it is not Gilman's commitment to sociology per se that marks her out as a classic. Rather, it is the pursuit of such a vision in and through her critique of existing gender relations and ideologies of domesticity. First, she presented a sweeping indictment of the dominant 'androcentric culture'. Given the extent of progress in other respects, Gilman argued, how extraordinarily primitive it was that social values and mentalities were so pervasively governed by the ethos of man the hunter and man the fighter. Prevailing notions of strength, health and sport, of good business practice, of educational success, of the appropriate toys to give to children and the right clothes to wear, even ideas of moral virtue, these were all definitively cast in the image, or else in the shadow, of the thrusting, selfish, rivalrous, competitive, instinctive, individualist man in the wild. In a culture so androcentric, it had become almost unthinkable that social life could be led according to a more collective, sharing, creative, supportive set of norms.

If we look at a cultural realm as important as religion, Gilman insisted, it is 'his' religion rather than 'hers' that dominates. For example, the image of God Himself as a judge and father; the presentation of Christ more in terms of his all-powerful resurrection than his loving life; the intimate association, from the Garden of Eden onwards, between women and sin; and the obsession with being saved and rewarded in the afterlife (the Happy Hunting Ground in the sky) rather than with what is sacred to us all in the present – all this is religion structured by patriarchy, not social religion as it should be. Gilman herself affirmed a kind of 'vitalist' metaphysic, a secular but spiritual outlook in which 'God' was best translated as the Lifting Force of the universe, the flow and pulse of life through us all, pushing us to create and to act.

Searing though her critique of masculine culture was, Gilman did not exactly blame men. If men were certainly rather primitive and laughable, at least they did things in the world. For Gilman this sense of participation in the force of the public world was the mark of modernity and the hope for development of the human species as a whole. Women, by contrast, are enveloped in a crushing culture of service, sacrifice and neediness. And in order to bear this unworthy position, a whole fantastical domestic mythology had been constructed, revolving around our supposed universal need for family privacy and intimacy, and the general success of mothers in building a safe haven for children in the home. But sociologically this was all nonsense: home was a place of strife and bickering, women were not particularly good cooks or mothers, children were not particularly well nurtured by instinctive protectiveness. The sheer amount of time taken up by cooking and cleaning guaranteed women's exhaustion, narrowed their aspirations and eroded men's affection for them. In one of her many effective rhetorical tactics, Gilman imagines the reaction of the extraterrestrial sociologist to all this. Such an observer would find it both 'touching and pathetic' to see women 'bear and rear the majestic race to which they can never fully belong'. Witnessing women's lives and talents so utterly sunk in the service of others, our visitor would surely head off back to Mars, 'marveling at the vastness of the human paradox'.

For Gilman, the primary cause for the modern gender malaise was the 'sexuo-economic relation'. Astonishingly, she reflected, it is in the human species alone that the female's very livelihood is bound up with her willingness to perform sexual services (encompassing both sexual gratification and mothering). Fulfilling the sexual functions totally absorbs women's whole identity, and this is transmitted down the line to the children, of both genders. Men, for their part, do things in order to attract their partners initially (which Gilman thinks is fine enough – everyone should be primarily *doing* things), but thereafter have to get things (money, property) in order to keep their women. And in order to be kept, and ornamented, women cease to do anything in the wider society. As fleeting attraction fades, men become nothing but the economic environment of women, and their feeder. Women use their sex initially to attract the best provider, thereafter fulfilling sexual functions simply in order to live. In this way, Gilman drew a strict parallel between marriage and prostitution.

Gilman was not a deterministic evolutionist: these

current species characteristics were a social construction rather than some nature-given necessity. Where evolution worked unalterably *on* the other animal species, its principles work *through* us, she argued. Through will, intelligence and cooperation, we can in fact accelerate the evolutionary process. Instead of the utterly dysfunctional domestic division of labour whereby the men work to provide for the family and the women look after the home, an advanced division of labour would take many routine cooking, cleaning, child-rearing, health and educational tasks out of the home altogether and into the hands of those who excel and delight in such specialist roles. The mass of women would then be enabled to play their own part in the social collective, and have time and energy to pursue loving and creative relationships.

Like all candidates for classic status, Gilman is a suitably controversial figure. Her work has been found relentlessly moralizing, and lacking in precise empirical and theoretical detail. Feminists today might question Gilman's commitment to rationalist notions of science, her scathing dismissal of psychoanalysis and her firm defence of monogamy. Her reticence about matters of sexual desire and expression, too, has been considered problematical, not least given her own attraction to women, and her awful, depressed experiences of family life (captured movingly in the short story 'The Yellow Wallpaper'). Finally, in her concern to secure the upgrading of the species, Gilman supported the sterilization of people considered hopelessly defective, and proposed that the problem of the demoralized Negro underclass could be solved by dragooning them into a state-organized army-like task-force.

Du Bois

While Gilman and others, like South African socialist feminist Olive Schreiner (1855–1920), were extending the sociological idea of structural relations by forefronting sex and gender, African-American writers like W.E.B. Du Bois (1868–1963) and Anna Julia Cooper (1858–1964) were doing the same for race and ethnicity (Cooper acutely posing the question of the intersections between race, class and gender). Like Gilman, Du Bois wrote in different literary genres and pursued a full life as a political figure and journal editor. Like her, he also clearly identified with the sociological profession. But Du Bois was unlike Gilman not only in being anti-racist and black, but in covering similar topic areas – domestic life, single mothers, the role of religion – in a more deliberately empirical way. Indeed, he expressed a dislike for 'armchair theorizing' and 'car window' sociology. In his work with students in Atlanta University's 'sociological laboratory', and in his pioneering single-hand study of communities in south Philadelphia, Du Bois brought together huge amounts of survey data, personal interviews and participant observation to document the real situation of the urban African-Americans that were perceived to constitute a major social problem and a major threat to social morality.

The purpose of such endeavour was clearly theoretical in the sense that it was designed to de-naturalize and de-mythologize virulent views about the way black Americans lived and thought. Instead of confirming the image of a homogeneous, immoral, criminal and lazy subterranean lifeworld, Du Bois showed that the people of Philadelphia's Seventh Ward were by no means all of one kind. This line of thought was fully and deliberately in conformity with the sociological idea of increasing differentiation and individualization in modernity. In other studies, Du Bois drilled back into the countryside to show that significant degrees of differentiation existed even there, decisively cutting off the ex-slaves from their African cultural roots. Having established the wider than expected variety of types, Du Bois did not hesitate to note with disapproval – in the manner of Charles Booth and Henry Mayhew's studies of London's 'dangerous classes' – the 'loafers' and the wasters amongst young blacks, and the lines of 'shameless' black girls putting themselves out to prostitution. Correspondingly, he played up the fortitude and worthiness of the many respectable sorts, striving to make a decent living and raise their families well. He also emphasized the surprising degree of hybridity in these communities – racial intermarriage and cultural mixing amongst Negroes, whites, Italians and Jews.

An important strand of this work was to emphasize the role of religious sentiment and practice, and its diversity. Some families retained strong attachment to traditional African spirituality and magic/voodoo, others rushed to Baptism and Methodism. Another book on the black churches by Du Bois, based on 100 different congregations, demonstrated that religion uniquely met a need for community building and mundane structured socializing – just providing a safe and convivial place to hang out. Religious congress had also stimulated some of the most vibrant music America had ever known (Negro spirituals, blues, jazz). If, under a rationalist lens, there may have been some flamboyant irrationalities within these subordinate worldviews — their animated excitations or supernatural fears — Du Bois's point was that these things played a crucial part in the healing and sustaining that black people needed as they navigated the tough transition from abject slavery to modern knowledge and freedom.

As well as boldly proposing that 'the problem of the Twentieth Century is the problem of the color line', Du Bois was amongst the first to try to give a non-naturalistic specification of the concept of race itself. He posed it instead as a compound concept, based on a number of factors rather than just one — biological inheritance. He felt there probably had to be an element of that, but other considerations were vital, too: a common history, spiritual resources, material conditions of life and a language of political striving. Thus, whilst race had little or indeterminate scientific meaning, it was a powerful social frame of understanding. Sociologists today would see this argument as replacing the concept of race with the broader one of ethnicity.

In addition to highlighting and defining the sociological significant of race, and the debunking of racist stereotypes, Du Bois theorized black subjectivity — the sense of self. As with any human being, black selves are the authors of their own thoughts and actions, but they also simultaneously see themselves through the gaze and value-judgements of the dominant white culture — having to over-prove themselves in doing anything good; constantly conscious that any perfectly normal slippage of behaviour or attitude will reinforce the stigma of inferiority. Within one self and one (black) body, Du Bois reflected, there were two warring souls, sometimes fighting for supremacy, always yearning for harmonious reconciliation.

This account of the 'double consciousness' of 'black souls' was derived to some extent from Hegel (Du Bois studied for two years in Germany – where he met Weber amongst others). Hegel depicted the philosophical nature of self-consciousness in terms of a 'master-servant' relationship. For Hegel, consciousness inherently aspires to subordinate the external world to its own operations, so that reality comes to be seen as the product of consciousness, not the other way round. This can only come through the recognition of one's own selfhood by another striving consciousness. However, no two consciousnesses are equal; they are engaged in a mutually dependent struggle for recognition and superiority, and inevitably there are winners and losers. But the dominant self and consciousness still needs the recognition of the subordinate consciousness. In fact, the master, whose dominant status is duly acknowledged by the servant's consciousness, actually depends more profoundly on the latter than the servant's consciousness depends on recognition by the master. This is because the status and identity of the master is virtually nothing without the obedient recognition, and the goods and services, of the servant, whereas the servant has an independent relationship to the external world through work, giving his consciousness a certain objective standing. He is thus in a position to partially withhold full recognition of the master even whilst playing out the subordinate relationship. Du Bois's key move was to draw upon this abstract philosophical account of the growth of self-consciousness to give an optimistic reading of the subordinate experience of ex-slaves in the new America.

Du Bois has been questioned for his elitist proposal that the 'talented tenth' of young black people should be singled out and trained for educational and political leadership; and for his later turn to Soviet communism and a Pan-Africanism influenced by that. He has been regarded as too empiricist to be a great sociological theorist, and his disdain for some aspects of ordinary black lives has been characterized as pandering to the values of the white establishment. A particularly interesting issue is whether Du Bois could be described as excessively Eurocentric. In his eloquent essay of 1900, 'The Spirit of Modern Europe', Du Bois argued that the great ideas that were born in Europe – freedom, justice, authority of government, systematic knowledge and the continuity of human organization – were indispensible to our best social future, even though in practice these ideas had been sullied by European colonialism.

In sum

Simmel: he both extended and counteracted the concerns of the classic European macro-sociologists, highlighting the cultural, subjective, 'numerical' and 'sensational' aspects of social interaction.

Gilman and Du Bois: whilst retaining allegiance to social Darwinist and European perspectives, they powerfully disrupted the dominant sociological norms by bringing into empirical view, and theorizing, the marginalized experiences of women and black Americans, respectively.

Interchange

Question:

So that's three founders, three classics and three other classics. Presumably there are yet others that we should check out?

Response:

Of course. Just to pick out three more of the dead white men, Vilfredo Pareto (1848–1923) was distinctive in pushing sociology towards the style of explanation prevalent in academic economics, in which he was also expert. Pareto's specific sociological interest lay in the psychology of power and the basic relationship between 'derivations' (ways of consciously thinking and arguing) and 'residues' (instinctive or cultural responses of a non-rational sort).

Ferdinand Tönnies (1855–1936) struck a balance between Marxist and Durkheimian themes. His main work appeared before Durkheim's and the two had a subsequent altercation about whether or not Tönnies's key distinction between pre-modern *Gemeinschaft* ('community') and modern *Gesellschaft* ('society') was approximately the same as Durkheim's distinction between mechanical and organic solidarity.

Gabriel Tarde (1843–1904) has been hailed as the direct foil for Durkheim. Tarde rejected the very notion of 'society' as being too vague and holistic, and he questioned the idea of necessary social development that was so prominent in other classical sociologists. Instead, for Tarde, social interactions and occurrences should be regarded as necessarily contingent associations. They need not have happened, and they need to be grasped in and of themselves, and not referred to general commonalities across time and place.

7

American hegemony

In the early twentieth century, as noted, the positive elements in modern society – its 'push' – seemed to have moved across the Atlantic to the economically booming and culturally upbeat American setting, however beset it was with racism. Sociology followed, in spirit and numbers, as many European intellectuals sought to escape fascism by migrating to the United States. There were accompanying shifts in sociological bearings. The change towards 'micro-sociological' concerns was one of these. The understanding of personal identity rather than structural constraints seemed in keeping with the driving message of America's young capitalism: that individuals can achieve what they want, given sufficient determination to succeed.

The American sociologists of the early twentieth century took on board not only Spencer's sense of evolutionary development, but something of his ideological optimism on the role of individual self-interest and active responsibility. It was thus held to be part of structural social development itself that structural constraints were less determining of interaction than once they had been. The pragmatic question facing

Western civilization was how, systematically, to encourage mobility and diversity amongst individuals and social groups, while at the same time coping in a realistic piecemeal way with the social problems inevitably thrown up by such a go-ahead melting-pot society.

Pragmatist interactionism

Simmel, as well as Spencer, was a major influence on sociological work in the United States in the early twentieth century, and their ideas, in turn, were blended with the philosophically pragmatist outlook whose leading light was William James (a founding figure of psychology, too). Pragmatism in this context meant taking a back seat on ultimate philosophical questions such as the meaning of life, the nature of world history and the search for absolute truth, and concentrating instead on how moral and symbolic worlds are constructed on a 'local' basis, in the here-and-now. Charles Cooley was one sociologist who developed this socio-psychological orientation with his notion that we are all 'looking-glass selves': we imagine ourselves largely according to how we think others see us. For instance, we may be ultra-sensitive to our cowardly traits in the presence of an ostensibly brave person, or think of ourselves as stupid in the company of an apparently clever person. Another soundbite of the time was that 'if men define situations as real, then they are real in their consequences'. In other words, 'society' does not pre-exist our own subjective and inter-subjective construction of it: we literally *create* society in and through mutual definitions of our situations.

An important theorist to grasp social selfhood in this neo-pragmatist manner was George Herbert Mead (1863–1931), who in his teaching at the University of Chicago founded what was later labelled the 'symbolic interactionist' tradition in sociology. Mead pointed out firstly that it is the use of language as a symbolic medium that distinguishes human interaction from that of other animals, and that language is essentially and creatively a social practice. When we talk together, we always simultaneously put ourselves in the place of the other as well as expressing ourselves. The social self is thus uniquely positioned as both the subject and object of consciousness. We anticipate certain responses from the other person, assuming a shared understanding, and we work towards confirming that shared understanding as cooperative beings that project into the given situation. Even when we are conducting an internal dialogue, trying to think about what it is that we think, we are, according to Mead, engaged in an interpretative process between the 'Me' (the part of me that others see) and the 'I' (the part of myself that reflects on how I am seen by others).

Drawing upon many processes of socialization, and innumerable situations of social action and interaction, we become instinctively aware of how society has formed us, and of what society expects of us. Mead termed this socialized part of the interactive self the 'generalized other' – the tangible presence of social norms within each of us, which is partly mediated by our attachment to 'significant others'. For example, we learn to see the reactions and influences of our particular parents (or friends, or church minister) as representing the general role of parents (or peer groups, or the church) in this type of society.

After Mead, symbolic interactionism developed a number of different currents. Some 'Chicago school' advocates felt that its essence lay in a socio-psychological analysis of particular situations, believing that you couldn't usefully generalize beyond what Mead had said about the meanings of interactions. Instead, you had to take it situation by situation, adopting an essentially qualitative approach to sociological understanding and seeking to show how we individually and collectively respond to the way in which we are labelled. Others (e.g. the 'Iowa school') felt that the prevalence of social meanings, even in particular situations, could quite effectively be measured and generalized in a quantitative way. Perhaps most important of all, the impact of the symbolic sociology of Mead and others was to fully establish micro-sociology as a going concern, such that society is to be seen as a constructed, negotiated reality reproduced and altered on an everyday basis by individuals. By the same token, society is not to be seen, in the classical manner, as a thing-like general abstraction, having its own laws of motion like some strange planetary object.

The Chicago school era of sociology was not only concerned with identity and interaction but also with perceived social problems, which in places like Chicago would have been plain for all to see. The rapid growth of American cities and the almost natural way in which the new metropolis grew generated a spread of very different social zones and subgroups – the docks and factory areas, business districts, shopping areas, residential streets in the city centres, ethno-cultural districts, underclass domains, outer suburbs and so on. The egalitarian liberal ideology of the New West allowed marginalized groups – women, African-Americans, the labour movement, European immigrants – to stake a claim to be included in the pluralistic society. But social conflict and deprivation, reflected in strikes, racist violence, street crime and child neglect, demanded a more progressive, collective response if these social problems were not to overwhelm the democratic potential of the country.

The extent of these social problems needed to be documented, and remedies for them found, through a steadfast reforming attitude that pressed for remedial action in whatever practical form it came, whether through the state, religious organizations or private charities. Some sociologists were prominent in the churches, and received some reform-oriented funding for their grass-roots research. As a result, the previous dominance of sociological theory within the discipline gave way to a rather different and more relevant professional image: sociologists were people who undertook empirical projects designed to identify and help solve the social problems that characterized the new 'ecology' of cities. In a journalistically lively way, they described the meanings and interactions prevalent amongst street gangs, down-and-outs, the new professions and the onion-like structure of the spreading urban zones.

The reforming ambience of American thought in the first half of the twentieth century is exemplified in the role that the sociological feminists who were dubbed 'the women of Chicago' played in practical and theoretical debate. The Chicago women shared the same broadly liberal-progressivist views as the Chicago men, but their work was more directly activist, centred outside university circles, in community projects and reforming campaigns of various kinds. In that context, rather than in the academy, sociological knowledge and personal experience could properly be brought together. The leading figure in this feminist political sociology was Jane Addams (1860–1935), whose interactionist perspective highlighted the fusion, within social experience, of supposedly separate rational and emotional elements, and whose political motivation was to insist that the mission of modern democracy could not be fulfilled unless it was fully socialized; that is, given a firm grounding in a more equal, participative and inclusive society. Democracy for Addams and her feminist circle was not the formal matter of legal rights and voting at elections, but rather the hands-on, on-going business of people working responsively for and with one another in all spheres of life – in the family, in education, in the neighbourhoods.

Talcott Parsons

During the period we have just looked at, sociology had become, perhaps for the first time, an established profession, attuned to considerations of modern social selfhood, oriented towards social problems and increasingly skilled at large-scale empirical research. However, the turbulent condition of Western society disallowed any new, confident sociological big picture, outside Marxism, prior to the 1940s. Only then was the tide of Nazism and fascism in Europe beginning to be turned; only then were the economic depression and the crisis of capitalism being significantly reversed (largely through the boom of the war economy); and only then did the very notion of society begin to seem legitimate once again, after years of state dominance within the fabric of civil society. With the United States least affected by outright political tyranny, and with the new Cold War between the US-led West and the state-Communist bloc of nations during and after the Second World War, the status of liberal capitalism as the upside of modernity needed fresh articulation.

Through the 1950s, with politics and social conflict certainly no less pressing on the concerns of intellectuals, Western academic life nevertheless became more institutionally consolidated as a relatively separate domain of reflection, research and scholarship. A corresponding sense of specialist expertise was cultivated, often defined and developed, whether rightly or wrongly, as modes of thinking which are not overtly ideological. Subjects in the humanities and social sciences became increasingly technical rather than openly value-laden. Professors of literature, for example, became meticulous about the way that properties of metaphor and rhetoric defined what it was that cultural works had to say. Social scientists took advantage of rapid advances in computing to develop sophisticated quantitative research methods, leading to a new sort of scientific image fit for the 'cybernetic' age.

This expert professionalism, and image thereof, reflected the view that moral and political values (which no doubt everyone had) should be kept separate from the state of the facts and the workings of the systems. Leading social commentators were willing to accept that they had some kind of ideological orientation, but this was usually couched as liberalism and pluralism, the sort of viewpoint that was felt to be more low-key and 'balanced' when compared to more 'extreme' ideologies. In the context of a mobile and relatively prosperous society, those strong ideologies were held to be going into decline, along with the more divisive, destructive social conflicts of previous times. This was the period, then, in which 'the end of ideology' and 'the affluent society' were announced and celebrated.

Within sociology, such intellectual shifts were reflected in an intriguing way in its most prominent figure through the 1950s and 1960s, Talcott Parsons (1902–1979). Parsons sought to create a new style and a new consensus in sociology, as if to match the growing sense of consensus and stability in the wider postwar society. He wanted to show how all stable modern societies functioned in a more or less well-integrated way and, within this, to play up the role performed by the 'central value system'. Parsons was on a mission, and pursued it with impressive drive; but it was a curiously bloodless mission. His starting point was to recover what he felt had been lost in the passage from Europe to America, namely the place of 'grand theory' at the heart of sociological science. He felt that the pragmatism and empiricism of Chicago-era sociology had become too descriptive, and that a new synthesis at the analytical foundations of sociology was called for. And Parsons developed an appropriately different manner of composition to match the update and upgrade he was proposing. Impersonal and distant in tone, his work is full of stipulated definitions, box and flow diagrams, acronyms, and systems and sub-systems all neatly nested into one another.

Parsons reviewed the contributions of various older classics, singling out Durkheim and Weber in particular as genuine founders of the discipline, explicitly ruling out Marx. What those two did was set the fundamental terms of the 'theory of social action' that all good sociology should be connected around. The task of redefining and completing this project fell to Parsons himself. From Weber he took the priority of analysing social action as always a voluntary matter, seeing the Marxist alternative as too deterministic by far. But Parsons's individualism was meant to go decisively against the kind of utilitarian, self-interested notion of individual action that he thought underlay the modern science of economics, which itself, he claimed, completely undermined the very idea of sociology. Instead of people being driven, consciously, by material interests and a firm menu of instrumental preferences, Parsons extended Durkheim's sense that our actions are always morally and collectively orientated. Unlike Durkheim, though, Parsons felt that norms and values, whilst socially derived, were not externally constraining on us in contexts of decision. Rather, they were internal to the very meaning and logic of the action-situation itself – or what Parsons termed the 'unit act'. In the unit act, the agent selects specific goals according to the material means available to achieve them, guided by the norms and values in the wider culture that typically attach to those goals and means.

In his later work, Parsons sought to develop a general analytical scheme that could apply both to something as individual as the unit act and to the workings of the social system as a whole. Human systems, at all levels, have their own stand-alone rationale, but also need to be seen as forming part of some larger system, and as having component sub-systems themselves. Thus, for example, the social system, which contains various sub-systems, is also conceived as a sub-system of something larger, namely the 'total action system'. And according to Parsons, all systems large and small must meet certain 'functional prerequisites'. They must *adapt* to an external environment; steer themselves by *goal-directed* decisions and strategies; be *integrated* by way of various rewards and sanctions; and be underpinned by latent value-orientations or attachments that will meet our need for a degree of existential and moral stability within a system. Parsons sometimes gave the name of *latency* to this fourth dimension, and sometimes he called it 'pattern maintenance'. Taken together, these four dimensions or sub-systems made up Parsons's famous 'AGIL' model: 'A' for adaptation, 'G' for goal directedness, 'I' for integration, and 'L' for the latent attachment and pattern maintenance element.

We can therefore visualize the 'total action system' as a square or four-pane window with the four AGIL letters arranged clockwise at the corners. 'A', the adaptation sub-system, is top left; this is the organic or organismic sub-system — referring to that biological aspect of human existence centred on survival, reproduction and our other 'animal' needs. Then moving across to the top-right pane/square, we have 'G' the goal-directed aspect of the total action system, named by Parsons as the 'personality' sub-system — referring to the fact that humans are intentional creatures constantly devising ways of getting what we need and desire. But getting what we need and desire is potentially anarchic, so the 'social system' is what provides coordination of collective behaviour, through all sorts of institutions, rules and controls. 'I' for integration is thus situated in the bottom-right square/pane of the total action system. Finally, in the bottom-left pane/square we have latent attachment to pattern-maintenance, which is reckoned by Parsons at this very general level to belong to the realm of culture in human life — all the things we value and delight in, the aesthetic and normative aspect of existence.

Now, let's zoom in on the social system itself, and think of it as the only square we are looking at, divided into its own four component squares/panes with the AGIL letters once again at its corners. Parsons tells us that the adaptation sub-system of the social system (top-left square) is represented by the *economy*, the goal directed sub-system is *politics and government*, the integration sub-system comprises various mechanisms and institutions of *social control*, and moving round to bottom-left we have normative commitments and *value-orientations*, the role of which is to resolve or manage residual tensions that could easily break out as a result of the operation of the other sub-systems.

On the same basis, we can once again zoom in further, for example on the bottom-right square of the social system, and think of the *law*, for example, as one major institution of social control fulfilling the 'I' function. (This example is improvised

– Parsons doesn't quite put it like this.) Like any effective organizational form, the law must meet the four functional prerequisites at this lower level of the social system as a whole. It must secure its resources from the general socio-economic environment (adaptation, top-left); and it must specify and try to achieve certain goals (top-right), such as keeping the peace, delivering acceptable 'justice' and so on. Then, moving to bottom-right, the law must itself be well integrated through the kind of internal and external social controls and rewards that are typical of legal arrangements (the accepted status hierarchy of legal roles and law firms, ways of working that are regulated by external bodies). Finally, the institution of law must be sustained by the latent energy and commitment that comes, for example, from attachment to the view that without law we would descend into anarchy, that democracy could not be achieved without the 'rule of law', that there is equality before the law and so forth.

Although he confessed himself to be an 'incurable theorist', Parsons insisted that his various general theories were adaptable and concrete enough to offer strong guidance to programmes of empirical research, showing at every level how institutions were organized according to their functional prerequisites and tension-handling pattern maintenance variables. He also thought that, in modernity, there was a general evolutionary development in the typical *role-expectations* that grounded pattern maintenance. One aspect of this was the shift from the 'diffuse' to the 'specific' in social interaction. When visiting our doctor, for example, we only expect her/him to be concerned about our health and its remedy, not everything else about us. Nor do we expect doctors to get passionately involved in our lives, which would be inappropriate because it would go against our expectation of their 'affective neutrality' – there should be a proper sense of distance between us. And we would think it odd if doctors behaved in one way towards us, and acted completely differently towards others: this is evidence, in Parsons's terms, of 'particularistic' behaviour and values giving way to 'universalist' ones. The status of a doctor, moreover, is understood as a matter of merit and achievement rather than deserved or undeserved on the basis of ascribed characteristics – family background, size, colour, ethnicity, gender and so on.

We might note here that aspects of the modernist evolutionary shift that Parsons described seem less clear-cut today. For example, people often seem to want more holistic involvement from health and other professionals in their lives; and in multicultural postmodernity, the particularities of specific social identities are felt to require greater recognition than liberal universalism allows.

Overall, Parsons can be admired for the sheer ambition of his work, the consistency of his interpretations and the creative (if slightly odd) way that he went about tackling key sociological questions. But by the mid-1960s, Parsons's structural-functionalist brand of theory had been critiqued from all possible angles. It was accused of being both too abstract and too empiricist. It was accused of being too complex but also too simplistic. Parsons was attacked for having forgotten about *dis*equilibrium and *dys*functionality and the messiness of social change in his obsession to dissect how it was that societies hung together, more or less. He was thought to be too idealistic in terms of his ontological emphasis on norms and values. He was berated for creating a vision of conformist man; for underestimating the prevalence of social conflict; and for exaggerating the power of socialization. And he failed in his search for consistency, because having started off with a 'voluntarist' theory of action, Parsons ended up with an ultra-formulaic concept of society in which real human beings functioned as little more than cogs or ciphers.

Having been subject to this level of criticism, it was not surprising when reconsiderations of Parsons eventually surfaced, culminating in the promotion of the label 'neo-functionalist' by some sociological theorists in the 1980s. The point was made that Parsons was both philosophically sophisticated and scientifically knowledgeable; that he was not completely uncritical of capitalism and liberalism; nor completely neglectful of change, or conflict, or inequalities. Furthermore, in the work of Robert Merton, Parsons's contemporary, a more subtle version of functionalism was expressed. Merton drew an important distinction, for example, between functions that were 'latent' and those that were 'manifest'; and he also argued that it was not against the proper spirit of analytical functionalism to examine how deviant or dysfunctional elements in people's roles and subcultures could qualify the presupposition of societal integration. Above all, neo-functionalism reaffirmed the Durkheimian element of Parsons: even if they both were too optimistic about the normative potential of liberal, functioning modernity, their emphasis on continual processes of social differentiation and large-scale interdependency based on increased levels of specialist knowledge remained valid. And this perspective encourages us to see the production of social divisions not as due to a single principle of structural exploitation like class, but to a complex web of stratification in and out of the workplace.

In sum

In the older sociology textbooks, Parsons was routinely featured as the dominant presence in twentieth-century sociology. But Parsons's phraseology and mindset now strike many readers as very problematical, and his downfall is felt to be related to his implicit ideological alignment with the mid-century liberal capitalist consensus in the United States. That said, Parsons's theoretical style was both distinctive and intellectually interesting, and his formulae, despite being very abstract, did manage to generate insight into empirical situations and attitudes within Western late modernity. We can exactly reverse this train of thought for the brand of sociology associated with the 'Chicago school'. Once thought to be of significance, mostly, for its non-theorized, close-up observational focus of life in the neighbourhoods, interactionism has been repositioned as a compelling theoretical tradition as well. This is because of its alignment with philosophical pragmatism, its 'dialogic' approach to its research subjects and its moral commitment to 'local', bottom-up social agency.

Interchange

Question:

What are you leaving out of the story of sociology in the United States and elsewhere during the twentieth century?

Response:

A great deal. In the years of consolidated sociological professionalism, a whole range of sub-fields were explored and taken forward, and by no means all in Parsonian fashion: the theory of organizations and the professions, the sociology of crime and deviance, race and ethnicity, systems theory and the increasingly specialist interconnecting of Merton-style 'middle-range theory' with sophisticated quantitative methods pioneered by researchers such as Paul F. Lazarsfeld. Similarly, in the next chapter, my depiction of the post-Parsons phase leaves aside many theories of class, stratification and community; historical sociology; social network analysis; new accounts of nationalism and state elites; analytical sociology; 'the new institutionalism'; and many others. These cannot be incorporated into a short book of this kind in any manageable way, but can be noted as significant labels that you might engage with later.

8

Conflict, contention, synthesis

The period from the 1960s to the 1990s is marked by overlap and succession amongst a range of different perspectives in sociology, leading to the frequently heard claim that – for better or for worse – sociology is a 'multi-paradigm' discipline, a subject in which we agree to disagree, rather than, in positivist style, a potentially unified science with an established set of concepts and discoveries to its name. Both of these visions have something going for them, but there are various ways of striking a balance between them. For example, you don't have to be completely 'scientistic' to feel that sociologists could quite easily agree to agree a little more than they do, instead of instantly agreeing to differ. Many of the apparently stand-off debates between different perspectives and theorists tend to screen out a considerable amount of shared observation and understanding, even if many significant issues will never be harmoniously resolved. This is not exactly 'positivism', but it does express a concern to play up the 'positivity' of sociological work, giving more prominence to what has been achieved across the various perspectives to enhance our substantial knowledge of the social world.

From that point of view, our story of sociology in this book is neither the tale of a single unified tradition, nor an account of the many incompatible traditions. We might consider here the metaphor of a river system moving downstream, fed by different classic sources and later tributaries, connected and indeed braided together in various ways, yet containing many relatively distinct beds, rivulets, rapids, eddies and counter-currents. In this scenario, it remains to be seen whether these distinctive flows of academic energy terminate in a flat, broad, innumerably stranded delta, or a channelled confluent surge into the wider intellectual and political ocean beyond.

In any case, after Parsons, sociology certainly became more politically radical, recruiting in the late 1960s and 1970s large numbers of critically minded academics and students in the United States and Europe, and spreading a more subversive message – 'Challenge "common sense"! Challenge the ruling elites!' This was the time of disillusionment with the West's pursuit of the Cold War, which was seen as driven by the interests and conspiracies of the 'military-industrial complex' against true liberalism and democracy. The Vietnam War turned middle-class American youth against the perceived complacency or redneck conservatism of their parents' culture, and serious urban uprisings in African-American areas broke out, triggering outraged counter-reaction from respectable white society. Colonialism was ending, as many states in the Third World began to assert their right to economic and political independence and cultural autonomy. In this context, young sociologists were no longer asking, with Parsons, how society worked in sustaining cultural equilibrium, or how we could be more scientifically credible. Rather, they were demanding: whose side are we on?

Conflict theory

In this more radical vein conflict theory emerged to challenge the assumption that society generally tended towards integration and that a consensus around values had been forged in the contemporary West. On the contrary, by taking a properly historical perspective and keeping a sharper empirical eye on present reality, social order could be demonstrated to be a precarious, temporary thing, with considerable dispute over fundamental beliefs hovering just beneath the surface, often breaking it. Conflict theorists were still largely liberal pluralists, but they took the point of the aspiring radicals that the 'end of ideology' thesis was itself a manipulative ideology, suppressing difference and contestation among groups under the American Dream image of a homogenous, affluent, contented citizenry.

However, conflict theory in turn was felt to be over-generalized. In place of consensus as the magical key to every analysis, we now had conflict, but this all-purpose idea of conflict soon became tired as a slogan, and was anyway theoretically rather vague. It also turned out to be less conceptually and politically subversive than anticipated, for couldn't it be said that social conflict itself serves an integrative or functional purpose in society, by acting as a kind of safety valve which presents across-the-board upheaval?

Neo-Marxism

Neo-Marxism in particular questioned the pluralism that was shared by liberal functionalists and conflict theorists alike. For Marxists, critical sociology has to be about more than identifying and appreciating whole range of groups and the variegated conflicts that they happen to engage in; you have to say which groups are most powerful and oppressed, and you have to analyse such divisions in terms of the overarching conflictual logic of the modern capitalist system. This question began, and in some ways continues, to dominate debates in social theory: how far can analytical and ethical pluralism be taken before it starts to refer to so many things of apparently equal value that it becomes vacuous?

The greater rigour of Marxism in filling out exactly what social conflict meant found favour through the 1970s, despite the continuing shadow cast by undemocratic communist states governing in the name of Marxist thought. Some of the newly academicized Marxists (or 'neo-Marxists' or 'Western Marxists' as they were called) conducted their own stringent critiques of Stalinist tyranny and state control. Their work also emphasized, more than did old-style orthodox Marxism, the importance of culture and consciousness. The roles of politics and the state were deemed to be 'relatively autonomous' from the dictates of the capitalist economy and the capitalist ruling class. In other words, though capitalism might still provide the logic of the global economic system, the issue of just how it rules – whether in politics or culture – was felt by neo-Marxists to be a trickier question than previous Marxists had realized.

The 'superstructures' of society were not only to be regarded as arenas of contestation rather than wholly subservient to the needs of the ruling class, the very distinction that was doctrinal to orthodox Marxism, between socio-economic base on the one hand and cultural-political-ideological superstructure on the other, started to disintegrate.

Exchange/rational choice theory

Through the 1980s a pincer movement took place which led to a sharp decline in the position of Marxism within academic sociological rankings. From the more conservative side came exchange/rational choice theory. This tradition had a long pedigree, going back to the utilitarianism that Marxists and Parsonians alike felt to be unsociological because it largely disregarded the influence of social collectivities, their struggles and values. But in spite of this common criticism, exchange theory was envisaged as definitely encompassing sociological as well as purely economic forces and motivations, seeking also to incorporate interaction based around emotional reinforcement and social recognition, regardless of strictly material costs and rewards. Of course, if you entice me into doing something rather underhand in return for money or the promise of academic promotion, my behaviour might well be influenced by such straightforward material considerations. But, equally, if engaging in this exchange will cost me my colleagues' and students' respect, I might well refuse the offer. So exchange theory is certainly a form of behaviourism – it is how social actors actually respond (or not) to various sorts of stimuli that counts. But it is not exclusively economistic because value exchanges are included. Nor is it completely individualistic, since groups and nations can also be counted amongst the agents that deliberate on possible outcomes. Nor is exchange theory purely rational or deliberative, because unconscious motivations and desires can be incorporated within it, at least up to a point. Thus, all sorts of social interaction and conflict – class struggle, claims for ethnic identity, gender status, institutional trust, romantic love, family loyalty – can productively be considered as instances of social exchange and rational action, ways of strategizing in the particular social 'games' and bargains that are being struck and then broken all the time.

There even developed in the 1980s a style of 'rational choice Marxism'. After all, Marxism makes sense as an analytical perspective only if individuals generally follow the (material) interests of the classes to which they objectively belong. They struggle, bargain and play games with a view to maximizing such more or less conscious interests. True, the operation of liberal-capitalist ideology makes the pursuit of interest often less than fully conscious, but Marxists still envisage the gradual emergence of clarity, otherwise the dominant ideology could never be overcome. Thus, it is only when the mass of workers come to identify, and act upon, a higher kind of interest – the interests of enlightened, cooperative humanity as a whole – that the narrower interests of class conflict can effectively be superseded. The case was made, therefore, that Marxism itself conformed to what was perhaps the most coherent paradigm available in the social sciences. Against this favourable view, exchange and rational action theory are constantly bombarded with the accusation that they are 'reductionist' and 'methodologically individualist' to their core – society is envisaged as little more than the accumulated product of atomized individuals engaged in self-interested, strategic decision-making. This, it is alleged, leaves out everything in human behaviour that is non-rational and collectively constituted.

Meanwhile, even within avowedly radical sociological currents, Marxism came under attack for associating the notion of social interests exclusively with class interests, and for the distinction it retained between material interests on the one hand, and the exercise of power on the other.

Feminism

Feminism in particular challenged both Marxism and sociology in this way, arguing not only that the question of women's material and cultural subordination was being sidestepped in such conceptions, but also that the power-interest relationship itself was extraordinarily seamless. The feminist case went further still: women did not figure in the bulk of sociology's research findings; the key concepts of the discipline – class, bureaucracy, integration and so on – were themselves gender-blind; the canon of great thinkers contained no women; and the sociological career structure, as in all professions, was overwhelmingly organized around men's routines and mindsets.

Initially, the feminist critique was directed towards exposing this erasure of women, and of gender relations more generally, from social history and from the history of the social sciences themselves. Women were made more visible as social actors, and specifically feminist conceptions of the social structures of modernity were elaborated. Feminist concepts of patriarchy were enriched by conceiving it as involving several different spheres (home, work, violence, the state and so on) and, in the approach known as 'dual systems theory', Marxist notions of class were blended with gender as the key forces in reproducing structural inequalities. Marxism was still, however, regarded as having a limited — and therefore masculinist — understanding of modes of reproduction, tending to play down the importance of family structure and ideology.

But the parallels, as well as the differences, in analytical style within these combative sociologies were striking. Marxism and feminism, for example, shared more with structural-functionalist models than they were prepared to admit. Take the welfare state. Marxism generally views its development as something that capitalism needed at a certain point in order to secure the system's expanded reproduction and to give the working masses some kind of material and ideological stake in that reproduction process. And feminists, for their part, tend to see the welfare state as the institutional innovation that cements in place the idea and practice of the male breadwinner as central to the modern division between the public (male) sphere and the private/domestic (female) sphere. These characterizations of the rationale for state-provided welfare are broadly functionalist accounts: the significance of a social phenomenon is grasped by showing its role in the reproduction of an integrated system of one kind or another.

Of course, Marxists and feminists also saw the welfare state as the partially successful products of workers' and women's political struggles. These results were not gifts generously handed down by capitalists or patriarchs. So functionalistic social reproduction never happens independently of the actions and ideas of those involved. But then again, the same could reasonably be said of versions of Parsonian functionalism itself.

Micro-sociological currents

Following the earlier symbolic interactionist resistance to functionalism, a number of increasingly sophisticated micro-sociological currents came through in these decades as a kind of foil to the large-scale theorizing of Marxism, feminism and so on, on the one hand, and full- or neo-functionalism, on the other. Micro-sociologists, we should remind ourselves, do not necessarily want to dismiss altogether the big idea of social order; it's just that this societal order is a more cobbled-together matter than macro-sociologists imagine, something that is continually made and re-made by ordinary actors in everyday situations. One brilliant version of this was established by Erving Goffman (1922–82), who devised a distinctive, 'dramaturgical' perspective on social life in which interaction is seen as an extended acting metaphor. All the world is a stage, Goffman confirmed, and each of its component scenes, scripts and roles involve continual 'presentation of self' and the need to improvise. Sometimes what we do and say is 'front-stage' and explicit, sometimes it is 'back-stage' and covert. We have front regions and back regions in our interactive strategies. We 'save face', 'front up', 'play to the crowd', 'impression manage' and so on. Goffman thus invented a vocabulary all of his own.

Being a gifted, engaging writer, his narrative flair led his unusually numerous readers (for a sociologist) to suppose that in his portrayal of the psychological tactics that we all use, he was not terribly interested in 'theory', only in people and characters. But this is misleading, because all the time Goffman was trying to conceptualize as well as graphically depict the nature of the 'interaction order' and its different layers and settings of realization. Some of these settings are relatively (but never completely) unscripted, forming the fluid and changing context of everyday life in modern societies. But others are heavily scripted, seeming to allow no room at all for personal improvisation and alternative ways of being. Goffman called the latter 'total institutions', taking great interest in the way social reality was constructed in asylums, hospitals, prisons and the like. But without doubting the macro-sociological effects of power and control in such settings, part of Goffman's purpose in investigating total institutions was to reveal at the micro-level all manner of improvised assertions of identity, institutional game-playing and negotiations of role expectations.

Another important micro-sociological perspective, in which the achievement of social order and interaction is even more agentive and precarious than in Goffman, is 'ethnomethodology'. The main figure of ethnomethodology, Harold Garfinkel (b.1917), was a student of Parsons and shared the latter's intense interest in how social worlds integrate and hang together. But Garfinkel had no time for Parsons's increasingly macro-situated, evolutionary level of systems-theory interaction, preferring strictly to focus on the central role of talk, meaning and local routine among the ordinary members of social groups and settings. To that end, ethnomethodologists have drawn upon the philosophies of existentialism and phenomenology in developing an appreciation of the way that people stitch together their interactive commonality. They have cast light, particularly, on the complex way that conversations work. For example, for any verbal exchange to work, we have to 'take turns', so that when I say 'Hello' to you, in person or on the phone, you have to reply with a confirming gesture of some kind, prior to all subsequent content. Similarly, when buying things in shops, the default mutual assumptions are that the goods are going to be bought rather than stolen, and that we will pay the marked price for the product and not some other price altogether. Otherwise, our sense of collectively engaging in society would break down, and deviance would become the norm rather than the exception, which is almost a contradiction in terms.

Yet, for ethnomethodologists, it is important to see that at times very little separates workable interaction from a total breakdown of intersubjectivity, once the tacit operation of trust and local intelligence is questioned. This was shown through a number of 'breaching experiments', showing how frustrating and almost unintelligible things become when we systematically fail to confirm each other's expectations and roles in a defined situation. In these scenarios, shopkeepers for example were subject to random bargaining over the price of toothpaste; parents were exasperated when students started behaving in the family home as though they were paying guests in a hotel; and conversations were spoiled and rendered incomprehensible when one partner in dialogue persists in repeating the question 'why?' in spite of progressively helpful and detailed responses from the other partner, to the point where total bafflement and loss of purpose is experienced. The point was to show, provocatively, that social order is continually secured, and continually invites 'ontological' disruption, on this very specific and mundane level. Garfinkel was insistent that instead of being the 'cultural dopes' that he thought Parsons turned most of us into as carriers of the large-scale systems of social integration, social actors skilfully and caringly negotiated their social worlds all the time.

Post-structuralism

Another reaction against structural macro-sociology, but less intrinsically sociological as such, became known as post-structuralism. Structuralism (without the post-) was, for its part, something more than just large-scale thinking about the nature of society. Durkheim and Weber had done that, but they could not be called structuralist as such. Structuralism, rather, was the idea that society worked as a total system of meanings, and that to understand this theoretically, there had to be a kind of abstract 'code' to unlock its operational secrets.

The structuralists modelled the analysis of social phenomena on the way that language was reckoned to work. Language is the most general system of meanings that we have, and it possesses a rather remarkable abstract and stable quality, even though it changes all the time. This is because its meanings are generated through the way that the terms of language relate to one another – the idea is that they do not, in the first instance, relate to those real things in the world that we want to describe. Thus, the meaning of 'black' is not obtained by looking directly at the dogs, ink, skies, etc. that we need to characterize by colour. Rather, black gets its meaning from its abstract contrast with other colour terms, especially with white, as in 'black = not-white'. Similarly, the essential meaning of 'father' is established as not-mother, as well as not-son and not-daughter. So the binary codings (x = not-y) reveal the underlying logical bonds that connect meanings together, and such codings can be set out in clusters so that all the meanings that interest us can be coherently connected together.

With that analogy with language in mind, structuralists analysed a wide range of phenomena, from kinship systems and myths to fashion trends and magazine images. Sociologically, this approach was intended to help us grasp the full range of meanings of various social roles and ideologies. For example, when looked at for their social meaning rather than just their literal meaning, there are all sorts of important repercussions involved in the binary 'black = not-white' and 'father = not-mother'. More generally, structuralist sociology involves a vision of society as one massive 'code of codes', with particular binaries (x = not-y) clustered into ever larger contrastive categories, until the full spread of social meanings (father-son, husband-wife, old-young, West-East, capitalist-worker, black-white, in-group-out-group, deserving-undeserving and so on) are not only covered but also shown to be profoundly interrelated. Being a theoretical approach rather than offering a particular substantive account of the world, the structuralist style could be found, through the 1960s and 1970s, in a number of otherwise different sociological paradigms, as well as having a significant influence on quasi-sociological fields that opened up at that time, such as film studies, media studies and cultural studies. Until it was eclipsed by 'post-structuralism'.

Post-structuralism, you might say, stands to structuralism as ethnomethodology stands to Parsonian functionalism. It does not deny that society (or language, or meaning, or culture) is structured in various ways, but it actively resists the idea that such structures form a grand totality that stays stable long enough for us to grasp its underlying essential code. The point was not to revert to pre-structuralist social theories focusing on the conscious deliberate meanings of individuals/social people as such, because structuralism had undoubtedly revealed that much of what happens in social life is profoundly unconscious, and symbolic rather than simply material or intentional. Structuralism thus taught us to see social interactions as meanings, as 'texts' rather than outright natural or bodily realities.

But if structuralism showed that society is textual – governed by symbolic conventions and codes that we interpret and enact in various ways – it did not sufficiently appreciate that there cannot be only one privileged set of social meanings, or only one overarching logic that characterizes this (one) thing called society. Post-structuralists argued instead that no social meanings are ever stable, or entirely belong to their authors, or reflect society in any particular way. Rather, social meanings are always fleeting, contestable and multiple, and they can lead to all sorts of unforeseen adaptations and connotations. Equally, there are very many different types of discourse that we read as socially significant in some way or other. So, when sociologists seek to provide authoritative depictions of this thing called society, or indeed history, or even humanity itself, we must be careful not to take them at their word, but rather to take their enunciations *as words*, as discourses – something not to be proved or disproved per se, but rather something to be 'deconstructed' as a one form of uncertain interpretation amongst many others.

Many sociologists over the years have experienced, within the discipline, a kind of pulsing or oscillation between the kind of abstract depersonalized analysis that structuralism represents, and the more humanistic, observational mode of thought associated with approaches such as symbolic interactionism. And in truth, very few theorists have conceived their contribution as located definitively on one side or the other of the structuralism-humanism divide. Goffman, we have seen, was trying to take forward Simmel's project of adding a study of the 'nerves and tissues' that connect the principal 'organs' of societies, not replacing study of the latter. Garfinkel was trying to relocate the source and dynamic of societal integration, rather than to dispense with the idea of normative functionality altogether. And in the work of all the classics and the moderns that we have touched upon, what indeed makes them classics is some kind of attractive combination of the impersonal workings of social structure and the meaningful construction of social worlds by the living, struggling human agents themselves. So the quintessential sociological task, it seems, is not to pursue unilaterally the claims of structure against those of agency, macro against micro, function against conscious purpose, and so on; but rather to produce structure and agency synthesis.

Structure and agency synthesis

What tends to happen, however, is that whenever one perspective polemically engages with another, or whenever one sociological generation takes over from the previous one, what looked for one moment like a promising synthesis gets repositioned as an unacceptable one-sidedness, or an almighty mish-mash of conflicting priorities. The claim is thus typically put forward, for example, that Marx was not the totalizing theorist that he obviously aspired to be, but rather an economic reductionist; that Parsons, in spite of his almost heroic efforts to construct an even-handed approach to 'social relations' as a whole, was an out-and-out normative idealist; that feminist sociology, far from striking a difficult balance between its sense of all-pervasive patriarchal domination and its need to showcase the inspiring actions of women, is beset by contradictions between these two strategies. And so the search is on again for the next more adequate expression of synthesis, and for new terminologies that will really make it work.

Towards the end of the twentieth-century, these efforts toward synthesis included the 'structuration theory' of Anthony Giddens (b.1938) and the 'neo-functionalism' of Jeffrey Alexander (b.1947), prior to his switch into something very different going under the label of the 'new cultural sociology'. The mixing of neo-Marxism and postcolonial cultural studies was another kind of synthesis, and a more politically charged one, the most notable proponent of which is Stuart Hall.

Other projects of theoretical synthesis can be signalled for further investigation and appraisal: the blending of Marxism, interactionism and poststructuralist discourse theory by Dorothy Smith (b.1926) in her conceptualization of the textually saturated 'relations of ruling'; and the 'morphogenetic' way that Margaret Archer (b.1943) conceptualizes the relationship between the powers of social structures in relation to culture and consciousness, with Archer insisting at the same time on the autonomy and vitality of our reflexive subjectivity as individuals. But probably the most influential contemporary synthesizer has been Pierre Bourdieu (1930–2002).

Bourdieu conceptualized the 'social space' in which we all operate as composed of a series of 'fields' – the field of education, for example, or the field of art, the field of law, the field of economic relations and so on. Each field in turn is structured, for Bourdieu, according to positions and relationships that carry or generate various degrees of 'capital'. This includes economic capital, of course – wealth, material assets, money – but Bourdieu expanded the remit of the idea of capital to include things like connections and bonds between people (social capital), credentials and institutional positions (cultural capital), and also more intangible assets like prestige and taste (symbolic capital). Using this matrix of interrelated ideas, Bourdieu and researchers taking their cue for him have amassed a large amount of penetrating empirical research into the structure and experience of people positioned in these social fields, so his value, like all good theorists, is not just as a theorist.

However, Bourdieu, like all synthesizers, has been denounced for being one-sided rather than even-handed. The criticism is that he is too structuralist and deterministic – we seem to be rather too 'positioned' in his idea of power-laden social space. In response, defenders of Bourdieu highlight the centrality of his idea of 'habitus', which refers to the way in which we develop a way of coping and engaging with the world as filtered through all cumulative socialization, personal resources and dispositions. The habitus may well be a social product, but it is also the basis for the creative improvisation of our social positions, and it's something that changes all the time as we negotiate and strategize our way through the different fields and capitals. So perhaps we are not so abstractly determined after all. One could add that those who insist that people are totally free agents doing what they like and making up society as they please have perhaps found themselves operating in the wrong subject area. This is because sociology's basic rationale is in some significant degree intrinsically systemic, constantly pinpointing the combined sources of constraint and influence on personal action and choice. It is interesting, finally, to note that synthesizers like Bourdieu who are relatively more structuralist or systemic in inclination, are also more likely than those on the agency side to defend the idea of sociology as a scientific pursuit, albeit of a distinctly critical sort.

In sum

By the close of the twentieth century – not unlike the situation 100 years earlier – an enhanced awareness of complexity and pluralism characterized sociological thought, with many paradigms, many syntheses of paradigms, many methods and many purposes, both academic and political. Scientific up to a point in its findings and methods, sociology could not finally settle on any single big picture of what society really was about, or how social development was best to be conceptualized and measured. In a phrase associated with 1970s American theorist Alvin Gouldner (1920–80), it was recognized as an intrinsically reflexive discipline. That is, sociologists not only seek to develop analytical theories about the world, supported by empirical data, they openly acknowledge that sociological thinking itself is profoundly influenced both by our personal motivations and values, and by the events and social divisions of the social world we analyse. Yet, for all that sense of pluralism, sociologists also continue to see themselves as part of a common discipline, a shared progressive conversation and front of enquiry.

Interchange

Question:

Can the perpetual oscillation between structure and agency ever be resolved?

Response:

It probably can't, if we keep posing the sociological issue as though it was a version of the classically philosophical problem of 'freedom versus determinism'. In that model, agency is conceived as uncaused intentional intervention by our free selves in a world that is otherwise governed by objective laws and an overarching script that was devised before we thought we mattered. Sociologically, however, it is better to conceive of social structures (institutions, systems, groups, cultures) as having their own kind of agency as a result of their collective, but not exactly conscious, form; and to conceive of individual agents as themselves being complex structures of a certain kind, themselves composed of complex structures (brains, bodies, normative orientations, unconscious motivations). We are not fully free here, partly because our knowledge of these agency structures, and thus ourselves, is always limited and changing, and partly because we constantly interact with other structured agencies, both smaller and larger. As for larger scale societal systems, these have definite properties of their own, and a kind of agency, too, going well beyond the sum of individual inputs. But they don't operate independently of those inputs, so individuals and groups are never fully determined by them.

9

From the past to the posts

The last twenty years of the twentieth century were preoccupied by debates in social theory around the ideas of postmodernity and postmodernism, reflecting many of the long-standing issues and tensions we have already covered, and raising some new ones in addition. Following the issue of postmodernism, a whole series of other 'post-' phenomena and perspectives emerged.

Postmodernity/postmodernism

The thesis that we now live in a postmodern society draws on earlier suggestions about the coming of post-industrial society and the end of ideology. This signals a post-class or new-class world in which far fewer people work as typical proletarians in big factories producing mass goods uniformly for a mass market. Indeed, classical productive labour (factory production, mining, steelworks, shipbuilding, engineering, agricultural industries, etc.) has given way to innumerable sorts of 'service' jobs and information-driven occupations. Work is now more flexible in terms of both time and task; the economy is correspondingly more fluid, more design- and consumer-led; and indeed the market and its participants have gone virtual through enormous advances in home-based and mobile information technology, plus mass use of the internet and the World Wide Web. If we are not exactly in a fully post-capitalist economy, the capitalist economy has become radically 'disorganized' rather than planned, organized and delivered in the manner of Fordism. What are produced are no longer plain old durable *things*, but intangibles like emotional satisfaction, titillation and spectacular events to gaze upon. 'Material life' has therefore become an anachronistic way of referring to what economic production and cultural consumption now involve. Life is now so saturated by media projections and desiring fantasies of all sorts, that the very distinction between real social relations and our representations of them in thought and image is no longer sustainable. Instead, we live in a virtual network of hyper-reality, where innumerable signs and images proliferate and self-reinforce. (*Blade Runner* [1982] and *The Matrix* [1999] were movies that were said to capture something of this lurid, invented, captivating world of postmodern virtuality.)

As for parallel changes in social identity, instead of the solid and reliable self-identifications stemming from any one social position, we now recognize ourselves as cross-cut by a great many identities to do with age, gender, class, dis/ability, ethnicity, religion, sexuality, lifestyle, subculture, leisure practices, political and social commitments, and so on. These influences form a mosaic of social and personal discourses which voice how we choose to live our lives. Once-prevalent ideas like social class, in this context, have become inapplicable, so it is said — they refer to a stable world of work and identity that has gone. They are, in effect, 'zombie' categories, continuing in use solely out of sociological nostalgia for a stable, easily understood object of analysis. Postmodern society is more highly attuned to social and cultural difference rather than to social sameness. Amongst other things, this reflects the increasing multiculturalism of Western societies, but it also signals a world that is ever-changing, fragmented and constantly mixing new patterns of culture, ethnicity and creativity. A society, perhaps, where there is no such thing as 'society' at all.

What about postmodern politics? Just as we once had mass production and mass consumption, so we had mass politics: big and few parties appealing to the homogeneous voter, working out from their natural bases in particular and predictable class alliances. In this caricature, the working class voted for the parties of labour and the poor, while the privileged and aspiring classes voted for the conservative parties. But with the fragmentation and multiplication of social identities, and with the 'death of class', this form of politics becomes increasingly outdated. The old politics based on the nation state and fixed social positions and interests runs dry, and the whole idea of politicians being the representatives of social constituencies quickly fades. Politics becomes a career, increasingly subject to the dazzle and disasters of an ever more pervasive celebrity culture. In postmodernity, indeed, culture is the definitive aspect of society — politics, like socio-economics, becomes, in effect, culture. If social relations are inextricably mediated by their various representations, then ideologies and aspirations to make things better, and proposals to collectively organize for this purpose, become just another part of the flat universe of competing images and surface attachments. The politics of collective action loses its connotations of somehow being more deep or serious than personalized sets of opinions.

In epistemological terms, the postmodernist perspective was heavily influenced by poststructuralist thinkers like Jacques Derrida (1930–2004), who insisted that the modernist ideal of rationally and totalistically 'capturing' social reality in thought was either impossible or uninteresting. Postmodern philosophy continually emphasizes that the theories we invent are not neutral or objective or universal; rather they are culturally varied, multiple and diverse, more an expression of our desires and fantasies than an objective fix on how society essentially works.

A standard criticism of the whole postmodern scenario is that it relies upon a highly caricatured version of the modernist past, giving the false impression that no one in the old days engaged in leisure or consumption; that everyone was decisively located in a stable social class and always acted both predictably and en masse. Secondly, there are very obvious continuities between the modernist past and the postmodern present. For example, there is little conclusive evidence that a post-industrial, far less a 'virtual', economy exists in many societies of the world, or that work is hugely less important or routine for people nowadays, or that lifestyles are quite extraordinarily diverse, or that cultural understandings are totally different across different traditions and groups. Thirdly, it is contradictory initially to define postmodernity, as many theorists did, in terms of the inadequacy of totalizing 'meta-narratives' about history and society, only to go on to offer postmodernity itself as the new phase of society as a whole, the new totalizing concept that makes sense of things. Finally, part of the buzz around postmodernism was its reconceptualization of the boring old human self as a fragmented, multiple, shifting sort of creature, with no core personality or stability over time. But if taken out of proportion, this is a morally perilous idea, not an exciting one: truly split selves are not buzzy imaginative people; they are severely damaged psyches.

In this way, the postmodern agenda was thrashed out within sociology, with probably the majority being sceptical about its characteristic catchphrases and (especially) the sense of the utterly, inexplicably *new* that postmodernism transmitted. Related to this, sociological conservatives got annoyed when sociological enthusiasts for postmodernism joined in the chorus building up in some other academic disciplines that sociological ways of thinking were endemically too rationalist, and thus no longer capable of tapping into the pulse of the slippery, sliding, fluid, surface world that we now (supposedly) encounter. Being philosophical 'realists' by temperament, most sociologists also objected to the suggestion in postmodern thought that there was no meaningful way of even distinguishing between social reality, on the one hand, and our representations of that reality, on the other.

Sharp though this debate was, it did not stay completely polarized for too long, and various accommodations emerged. Eloquent sociological postmodernists like Zygmunt Bauman (b.1925) toned down their earlier warnings of how seriously destructive of conventional sociology the postmodern way of thinking was. And it simply couldn't be denied, on the other side, that some of the trends referred to in postmodern theory were actually happening to some considerable degree. So, around 2000, works began to appear that certainly contained aspects of postmodernist virtualism, but continued to hold on to aspects of traditional structural thinking as well. The account by Manuel Castells (b.1942) of 'the rise of the network society' in the 'information age' was one of these blended projects, attracting much debate. Was Castells, along with other sociologists such as John Urry (b.1946), really proposing that the fluid, boundless, globalizing virtual world could only be approached in a metaphorical way that defeated all conventional sociological attempts to measure, track and reason what was going on out there? On the whole, they were not. The point was rather that as well as carrying forward its good traditional analytical resources, sociological theory needs fresh resources, too, such as those derived from complexity theory.

Post-feminism

Over the last forty years, the impact of feminist thought on the sociological 'malestream' has been profound. True, that impact has not been as revolutionary as intended, but sociology has undoubtedly changed as a result of the politics of gender, in terms of what topics sociologists typically research, how the subject is taught and its general professional culture. As a result of this success, feminist sociologists no longer necessarily want to be talking all the time about the situation of women or patriarchy or gender. And not all views and studies in these areas of enquiry are necessarily feminist as such, though they have been made possible by previous feminist breakthroughs. 'Queer theory', for example, analyses and critiques behaviour and ideas that sustain what is called 'heteronormativity' – existing default assumptions about sexual desire, social behaviour and household organization. In 'queering' these assumptions, the point is not to make 'deviation' normal, but to trouble and disrupt the way in which all 'normals' invest in treating 'deviants' as strange and threatening. Sometimes the point might be to show that queers – the meaning of which is not restricted to sexuality – are more normal than you think; at other times the point might be to celebrate the departure from heteronorms. Meanwhile, feminist theorists themselves (such as Judith Butler [b.1956]) have broadened their concerns with the social construction of gender and masculinity to highlight the many different ways in which the social body is 'performed' in and through social roles and expectations of many kinds.

More generally, there is a concern to thoroughly re-link gender/sexuality with other social differences and divisions, and to explore their intersections. Partly this was as a result of women of colour and working-class women (and disabled women, Muslim women, indigenous women and so on) insisting that Western white feminist theory did not speak for them. But these developments are also related to the perception that, in some ways, gender power relations have changed in the wider society at large, and for the better. Many feminists would immediately point out here that we should not be misled by glib talk of girl power and the associated possibility that it is the boys/men who are now the victims. It is still women, after all, who do more in the home, even when they also go out to work; women's career structures still hit a glass ceiling at a certain level of seniority in many professions; average pay for women has rarely exceeded three-quarters that of men in any advanced economy; male violence against women has by no means ceased; and the increasing sexualization of young and not-so-young women still seems largely directed towards the male gaze – from an absurdly early age. Even so, the notion of post-feminism is interesting because there have indeed been notable shifts, partly as a result of feminism, such as the achievement levels of girls in school and university, the slowly altering norms of fatherhood and sharing of domestic responsibility, and in the forms of self-esteem attaching to gender identities.

Postcolonialism

Understanding modernity has been the central intellectual quest of sociology from its inception. But that central concept, modernity, involves associating a universal type or stage of society as a whole with concrete aspects of the place in which the first sociologists were located, namely Europe.

When sociologists first thought about what was 'advanced' in society, they replayed in their concepts the historical situation whereby the modern industrial order occurring in some European nation states was being exported to the rest of the world. And the assumption was that, economically and culturally, the model of society being exported was a good thing, and probably an inevitable one. So modern society itself gets to be associated with the achievements and the actions of the West, to the point whereby the Rest becomes simply the recipient, or the opposite, or the subservient. But the academic disciplines, along with world politics, have become progressively decolonized, so the traditional story of modernity has come into question. Instead, the notion of multiple modernities has taken hold, flagging up that the original Western model of modernity was just one model, and an ideologically particular one.

In developing these themes, postcolonial thought overlaps to some extent with postmodernism, which also undermined the sense that modernity was inevitable and progressive. But postcolonial authors tend to be critical of postmodernist theory, too, in that the constant 'deconstruction' of meanings is considered to be a kind of apolitical playfulness that in fact reflects just another side of Eurocentric metropolitan privilege. Postcolonial sociologists should perhaps be more interested in the way that indigenous and other peoples are still battling to have their significant differences from metropolitan and settler cultures recognized; to have their distinctive forms of economy, society, history and knowledge seen as legitimate and strong. The relentless pressures of the world capitalist system, economic growth, scientific and technological innovation, the spread of ideologies of 'freedom' – all these prevailing social norms and forces reflect the interests of the global North, not those of the global South.

Within sociology itself, postcolonial theorists contend, there remain deep Eurocentric biases, in terms of what sorts of thinkers make it into the sociological canon, and what is to be regarded as progressive and advanced. In qualification of these challenges, it should be noted that postcolonial thought is not necessarily *anti*-modern as such, or even anti-Western. Nor, for the most part, is it rejecting the core reference points of sociological thinking – social structure and systems, staged social change, scientific knowledge and so on. Rather, the point is to vigorously combat a parochial, narrow interpretation of these conceptions, and correspondingly to expand sociology's ability to listen to, and be changed by, the voices of peoples and groups to which it has customarily been inattentive.

Post-secularism

One of the striking features of recent times has been the revival of religion. In many parts of the world, religious movements such as Pentecostalism and Islam have spread rapidly, often in fundamentalist forms (whereby explicit theological tenets becoming thoroughly, unwaveringly embedded within both cultural life and personal conduct). Even in notionally secularized places, the relevance of religion to questions of science and lifestyle has been underlined, not least because of the presence and needs of migrant and settler groups to whom religion is felt to be central to their lives. These trends might strike sociologists as surprising, because ever since Comte and Marx the conventional sociological conception of modernity envisages the world as being steadily more 'disenchanted', in Weber's phrase: as people increasingly organize their lives around the scientific-industrial complex and getting on in the material world, the olden-days world of spirits and gods and miracles comes to seem irrelevant, and indeed even a little ridiculous. Secularism, in other words, is assumed to be associated with advanced society, religion with backwardness. Not only is this simple version of the 'secularization thesis' somewhat demeaning and insensitive to non-industrial cultures, but even within ultra-modern ways of life, religion and spirituality have not disappeared as such; they can strongly re-emerge within broadly secular society, if not always as large organized movements, then as the source of personal values.

Globalization and postcolonialism underline these points. Whilst in parts of Europe the secular outlook still seems to be gaining ground – previously strong Catholic countries like Spain and Italy are becoming less devout (less culturally embedded, less primarily motivating for individuals) – the heartland of modern capitalism itself, the United States, is significantly and even increasingly religious. When we look further afield at the range and depth of religions, in places that are also seeking to modernize, it seems plausible to argue that a 'de-secularization of the world' is taking place, in Peter Berger's phrase. Post-secularism thus refers to the different ways in which the balance between religion and secularity is being struck, and to debates in society generally about whether the supposed revival of religion is a 'good thing' or not. These debates have been acutely sharpened by events such as the attack by Islamicists on the World Trade Center in New York in 2001 ('9-11'), and by arguments in the United States and elsewhere about whether 'creationism' should be taught alongside Darwinian evolution in schools.

Post-secular points can be raised about sociology itself as a form of understanding. Even if we happen to be religious, we typically proceed when we are doing our sociology as if we are scientists, describing and explaining social phenomena in exclusively 'this-worldly' terms. The assumption is that the things that happen in society have social causes and not spiritual or divine ones. Such 'methodological atheism' does not mean that gods and spirits definitively do not exist, or that sociologists cannot be religious in their non-professional lives. But it does mean that the sociological standpoint brackets out such issues in order to focus on the societal logic of actions, ideas and structures.

Now, though, against this intellectual secularism, some religiously minded sociologists, together with philosophers like Jürgen Habermas (b.1929), who are today less methodologically atheist than they were in the past, are saying that it is time for sociology's secularist baseline to be re-examined and significantly softened. One response to this challenge is that sociology cannot be other than secular without utterly losing its identity and coherence as a way of explaining phenomena in the world. Another response says that post-secularism does not equate to the revival of religion as such; rather it is about seeking to pose the question of religion-and-secularity in new ways.

Post-democracy

Society has typically been imagined as national society – the people and institutions of a particular country, as defined by a certain territory, state apparatus, government jurisdiction, ethnicity or mixture of ethnicities, and cultural tradition. But nowadays, whilst the nation state has by no means disappeared, there are sub-national and supra-national organizations and identities of many kinds that are weakening the previously powerful association of 'the People' with the people of a particular nation state. This very idea of the people has been central to the values and concept of democracy. The democratic ideal has been that the people rule – democracy is rule by and for the people. But who are 'the people' exactly, and is there only one people? You could argue that this is just a figment of the liberal-democratic imagination. In reality, there are lots of peoples, groups with different traditions and interests, with not a great deal in common and with little likelihood of generating a spontaneous consensus on any major topic of societal concern. Instead of the democratic ideal of one people coming to express their common views by way of political representations through parliamentary elections and responsible government, we get a much more conflictual and partial view of how decisions are made and what kind of societal unity this represents. And how do we categorize the people of the entire world in our globalizing society? Is this one people, or many very different peoples?

One recent term used to describe the huge array of underdog peoples and groups across the world, the majority-made-up-of-minorities, is that of the 'multitude'. This new, postmodern and fundamentally global multitude is to be distinguished from the new global super-rich and governmental elites, so it is not a purely descriptive term: it tries to imagine that although there are many sociological differences within the global multitude, there might also be an overarching unity of situation and purpose with respect to the new 'empire' of chaotic and extravagant global capitalism. Another important – more concrete – idea is that growing numbers of people live in transnational communities; they see themselves as truly belonging to more than one nation, sometimes physically travelling between them, or sending significant resources from one to the other. There are increasing numbers of dual citizens. What, then, is the appropriate form of governance for societies containing these kinds of community? Seeking to take this question further, and to develop a style of sociological thinking that is adequate to it, some social theorists have claimed that in ethics and analysis alike, we must become resolutely cosmopolitan.

A further connotation of post-democracy is that governments, the super-rich, international organizations and multinational corporations have become so far removed from the lives and needs of ordinary people, and so apparently careless about them, that the demos, in turn, has begun to abandon the democratic political system altogether. In many places, over the long run, fewer people vote in elections, fewer people think politicians are trustworthy and fewer people are committed to being part of a societal community that feels overwhelmingly complex and alienating. Moreover, tendencies towards a 'surveillance society' have escalated. Policing methods and ways of counteracting terrorism, for instance, cease to be exceptional and routinely come to govern the lives of the peaceable majority too. In order to be more secure, it seems, we must give up more of our democratic liberties and accept that we are going to be ID'd wherever we go, have personal data about us stored and used by all sorts of companies and agencies, and constantly be monitored on surveillance CCTV. Not just terrorism, but anti-social behaviour of many sorts becomes targeted and stigmatized as socially dangerous.

A final aspect of post-democracy is the way in which all large public organizations and services have become corporatized, commercialized and run according to a shared new management ideology. Institutions like universities, local councils and hospitals are now run according to the needs of 'the brand', and accordingly operate in a streamlined, market-conscious, tightly budgeted and target-managed way. The 'business models' used to gauge efficiency and value in these settings have seen the development of a stand-alone jargon of delivery-assurance, and the promotion of leadership functions that are independent of substantive judgement and expertise. This new management culture runs counter to previous norms whereby the professional values and training of doctors or university professors or civil servants constituted the essential rationale of the institution, supported by an ethic of dedicated service amongst administrators. True, these older public-institutional styles were rather paternalistic and patriarchal in practice but, in principle at least, the vocational ethic contained a strong element of collegial and associational democracy. In the new public management discourse, the wellbeing and viewpoints of all employees are ostensibly declared to be highly important, but are tapped into chiefly by way of consultation and communication only.

Post-human/post-social

Classical sociology was based on the assumption that humanity could progressively gain rational control over nature, and that this would be more than half the battle against internal pathologies within society itself. Significantly greater collective knowledge, well-being and solidarity would then assuredly result. However, in spite of immense scientific and technological advances, our societal world appears to be spiralling out of control – and ironically this is partly because of such advances in science and technology. Most obviously, we have entered a period of severe ecological crisis and climate change, in which the end of the world as we know it is no idle, gloomy fantasy. Nature, in being radically socialized, is wreaking its revenge. Similarly, whilst technology develops relentlessly, its use for humane purposes seems destined to be thoroughly mixed, with disasters of all sorts – whether in terms of new medical hazards, disposal of dangerous waste, computer crash, genetic 'Frankensteins' and so on – routinely accompanying its benefits.

In this situation, sociologists are rethinking the excessive way that the 'human' has been sharply counterposed to the 'natural', and the 'social' counterposed to the 'technological'. To take the latter point, we have become more attuned to ways in which human and technical materials are being combined to form new types of being ('cyborgs') and to the development of 'prosthetic' life. Think, for example, of life-enhancing insertions of hardware into the human body not only following accident but to counteract normal wear and tear; and of how indispensable to our daily routines such things as computers, mobile communication devices, gym sessions, cosmetic surgery, painkillers, energy boosters and vehicles have become.

We might even reconsider the truism that only people can be social agents entering into social relationships. Is it not possible for example to perceive networks, organizations, computers, software and animals as possessing social agency? The perspective known as 'actor network theory' (ANT for short) characteristically advances such claims. The argument is that there is no such thing as 'society' or 'the social' as such – the social is really a whole concatenation of networks and 'assemblages' that link together human actions, physical materials, intellectual concepts, soft and hard technologies, and more indeterminate types of forces. For example, in understanding a bird flu epidemic, the agents – or 'actants' – include not only people, but also the birds themselves, the East Asian markets within which the condition developed, the conditions of the cages that contributed to the syndrome, the medical and transport technologies that aid and then seek to cure the problem and set various thresholds of 'healthy' and 'dangerous', the media that advertise the panic and fuel it, and the highly various opinions and announcements of all sorts of 'experts' and 'ordinary' people who become involved. Similarly, the university classroom situation cannot be classified under any one kind of human or material or ideational heading; it is an assembly or compilation of students, lecturers, PowerPoint presentations, the lighting system, coffee cups, the latest fashion, the breaking news, the ethos of sociology and the shoes on our feet. But it still has a distinctive kind of social force and unity to it.

The post-social concept also covers the possibility that the social systems that sociologists previously associated with nation states have become both more individualized and more internationalized. And systems or structures may no longer be the right terms to use at all, in order to grasp the highly mobile, fluid nature of global social forces and phenomena – information, images, media, migration, viruses and know-how. So there are two claims joined together here: that structures are melting into flows and scapes, and that global institutions are replacing national ones at the higher level, just as regional and local institutions are undermining the authority of the nation state from within.

Like the contentions relating to postmodern society, as tendencies these ideas are suggestive and credible. But they should not be exaggerated. For example, 2008 witnessed the most serious crisis in the global economic system for at least a generation, with a sharp wake-up call issued to bankers, governments and commentators alike. It was as if, for twenty years, elites had been in a fantasy-land, a bubble, in which nations' economies did not have to be connected very closely at all to material production and ordinary matters of worker employment and wages. Instead, they could merrily float along inside a purely virtual existence of their own, constantly generating more and more complex financial products, derivatives of derivatives, of the sort that would magically realize profits and enable more and more people to become fluid, mobile citizens of the global economy. With the threat of an economic depression on a scale not seen for sixty years, the concept of a social system organized around fundamental inequalities of resource and opportunity did not seem so passé after all.

Post-disciplinarity

Some of the trends we have been discussing – global society, multiple modernities, the complexity and interconnectedness of things social with things natural and with things technological – are reflected in the move towards interdisciplinarity within university study. Thus, just as sociology has opened out to the concerns and methods of other disciplines – politics, geography, history, psychology and so on – so those other frameworks of study have become steadily sociologized. Once upon a time the study of geography was about river systems, names of capital cities, population statistics and spatial coordinates; and politics was concerned with constitutions and party policies and the rise and fall of politicians. But now geographers and political scientists seek to examine questions of space and of power through the sociological lens of class and gender and ethnicity. Sociology was probably always more inclusive than other subjects, and therefore more intrinsically interdisciplinary – nothing, after all, falls outside the remit of 'the social'. Even so, sociology has taken on board new issues and methods coming from those other disciplines, also increasingly drawing on social psychology and psychoanalysis to fully grasp how emotions and 'affect' form part of all social situations.

Sociology has one foot in the humanities, at times drawing close to subjects like literature, history and philosophy. A significant development since the 1970s, for example, has been the rise of cultural studies as an intellectual project and academic field. Teachers of cultural studies have often characterized sociology as being insufficiently political and insufficiently attuned to cultural difference, but cultural studies derives much of its analytical bite and contemporary relevance from the considerable portion of sociological understanding that it undoubtedly contains.

There have also been significant movements towards a more serious interface between sociology and the natural sciences too. The sub-field within sociology known as science and technology studies has long been productive in that regard, and it seems increasingly vital that social scientists become knowledgeable about the 'harder' sciences if they are going to have anything relevant to say about the social consequences of, or the way social images and ideologies are embedded within, developments like genetics, bio-technology, nanoscience, climate change, artificial intelligence and computer systems.

A final issue about post-disciplinarity concerns the fact that we are now living in a time when the sheer amount of sociologically relevant data, and different types of data, is proliferating. Myriad institutions and firms churn out their own customer and public information, 'tag' it to ongoing profiles of people, lifestyles and postcode/zipcode areas, and manipulate it for their own purposes. Individuals, charities, think tanks, corporations, bloggers, Wikipediasts, Facebookers, consultancies, commercial agencies, newspapers, arts councils, community organizations, consumer groups, surveillance operations, reality TV in all its forms – all are in the data-production and data-analysis game. And, of course, segments and streams of socially relevant data now come in different material forms, media and shelf-lives (digital as well as paper, mobile technologies, private footage). This mushrooming of information alters the significance of sociology's typical sources of data (surveys and interviews conducted by themselves, plus government and other 'public record' documentation), indicating that professional sociology may be losing whatever monopoly it had on the quantity and quality of empirical records.

In sum

From postmodernism to post-disciplinarity, recent social theory has sought in various ways both to grasp what is genuinely new in social and political experience, and as part of this to revisit basic issues of understanding and ethics that have hovered just beneath the surface of social enquiry ever since the Enlightenment. The result is a rich menu of projects, in which elements of the old and the new, modernist and postmodernism mindsets, alternately clash and fuse together. And it raises the question of how best to imagine and practice sociology after modernism-versus-postmodernism.

Interchange

Question:

Why do we name all these developments as 'post-' something-or-other? This can be quite irritating.

Response:

OK, but just think: if we happened to be around as feudalism was breaking up we might have been tempted to use terms like 'post-medieval' culture or the 'post-manorial' economy just to register that something interesting and fundamental was on the go, but we didn't yet have the right name for it, in the absence of sufficient empirical understanding. We might not have had at our fingertips completely new ideas that super-seded the 'post' – such as 'mercantile capitalism', in this example. So the 'post-' serves as a useful holding operation, and sets an interesting agenda for research and debate. Also, the fact that its connotations are not crystal clear can be quite a good thing. For example, there's something in the 'post-' tag that suggests *coming after* the thing named, and perhaps also being *anti-* it (thus, anti-modernity, -feminism, -colonial-ism, -secularism, -democracy, -disciplinarity, -social/human, etc.). But the thing named still has a benchmark effect, suggesting that even in the 'post-' condition, there is a good degree of continuity and modification in play. It's seldom a matter of a total and utter break, though theorists sometimes cast things in that light to jolt us out of any intellectual complacency.

10

Twenty-first-century sociology

Right at the beginning, I introduced C. Wright Mills's notion of the sociological imagination and showed how this tried to strike a balance between the need for sociology to take as broad and objective a view of social events as possible, yet also be involved in the social and political changes of the day. In 2004, Michael Burawoy, President of the American Sociological Association at the time, gave an influential update of these themes. His discussion cascaded down through many national sociology associations around the world, creating an unusually focused, global and ongoing debate about sociology's pasts and futures. It is therefore appropriate to think about Burawoy's contentions as a way of drawing this brief presentation of sociology to a close. Considerations from the previous chapter will be woven in as we proceed.

The four sociologies

Burawoy articulates the broadest sociological quest as 'searching for order in the broken fragments of modernity, seeking to salvage the promise of progress'. This, we have already seen, is quite a familiar and inspiring idea, but perhaps it is an ideal that is becoming more difficult to sustain. For example, Burawoy shares the post-social observation that 'globalisation is wreaking havoc with sociology's basic unit of analysis – the nation state', and he shares the postcolonial feeling that coming to terms with this loss requires the de-parochializing of the sociology discipline itself. But the globalization process is wreaking wider havoc, Burawoy insists, producing vast inequalities in the world, and many inhumanities. So we are hardly in a post-class or post-capitalist situation. In such circumstances, sociology is still urgently needed in order to register, comprehend and contest such structural damage. How then do we manage to balance out the fact that sociological understanding has become very pluralized, with the need, somehow, to hold it together in the cause of social progress? Burawoy approaches this fundamental question by distinguishing between four types of sociological endeavour: public sociology, policy sociology, professional sociology and critical sociology.

Public sociology

If sociologists are not driven by pressing public and social issues, then the discipline is of no use whatsoever and will probably simply disappear. Public engagement is sociology's life-blood. It takes one form when prominent individual intellectuals speak out about the state of the world. Pierre Bourdieu, for example, in his later years (he died in 2002) was relentless in his condemnation of neo-liberal global capitalism and those academic trends that he regarded as its academic apologists. But Burawoy thinks that another form of public sociology is even more important. This is the thinking and data that is developed within activist social movements of one kind or another, fighting for a cause, and making crucial observations about the social world and the exercise of power. (Think of 'Make Poverty History' campaigns, green movements, anti-racism, etc.) Now, in a global pluralized world there is no single 'public'; rather, there is a multiplicity of publics, each open to contestation by various activist social movements. It therefore has to be accepted that many of these movements (political, religious, moral) will develop their own kinds of sociology, motivated by their own ideologies, with new 'organic intellectuals' coming through who are influenced by sociology but whose main commitment is to their particular cause.

Policy sociology

Engagement takes the form not only of social movement politics but also official policy development. Governments, funding bodies, charities and organizations all bring sociological knowledge and concepts to bear in devising new legislation and changes in institutional culture. For example, in a post-feminist age, there has been an effort to 'mainstream' gender equality, just as 'institutional racism' has been identified in a range of public bodies. Progressing these matters involves justifying, drawing up and seeing through definite legal and institutional guidelines, and policy sociologists accordingly channel their expertise into the nitty-gritty of administration and governance. In doing so, they accept that a major part of the sociologist's role is both to influence and to service 'clients' of one kind or another, including governments.

Professional sociology

By professional sociology, Burawoy means the basic academic education, research, culture and credentials without which sociologists are unlikely to become effective public or policy sociologists in the first place. Professional sociology is the space in which we acquire, debate and test our knowledge in terms of its scholarly or scientific validity, keeping somewhat in the background the more immediate political issues of the day and our own ideological inclinations. It is the space for developing, in Burawoy's words, 'tried and tested methods', 'evolving theories', and 'accumulated bodies of knowledge'. And it is where the various sub-fields of the discipline emerge and stabilize – the sociology of crime, sociology of leisure, sociology of religion, of the family and so on. Professional sociology is also where definite research programmes are developed under specific theoretical paradigms, which are then given the fullest run for their money, both empirically and conceptually.

Critical sociology

The role of critical sociology, finally, is sceptically to examine the foundations and logic of the dominant research programmes developed within professional sociology, and to promote new or revised perspectives based on more emancipatory principles. Critical sociology is positioned here as the conscience of professional sociology, just as public sociology is the conscience of policy sociology. Just as we run the risk, in policy sociology, of being co-opted by the interests of our clients, so professional sociology runs the risk of ossifying into the academic establishment, and indeed of bolstering the dominant ideologies of the era. But critical sociology exists to counteract this tendency, constantly questioning the findings and assumptions, and conservative implications, of dominant academic traditions.

In presenting his schema, Burawoy insists that whilst the four sociologies are different, and whilst he is making the case to give higher priority to public sociology, they are interrelated and interactive. For example, good public sociology still has to be good sociology; it cannot just turn into naked interest-group advocacy. Policy sociology should not be allowed to become the mere creature of the state. Professional sociology should not turn into insider-ism, such that under the dominant discourses, typical career patterns develop, status hierarchies kick in and loyalties are rewarded, with the consequence that some types of people are favoured and others excluded. And critical sociology must constantly guard against its own tendency to degenerate into mere dogma and excessive polemic. In this way, the 'pathologies' in each of the four sociologies can be compensated for by the corresponding virtues of the others. Overall, Burawoy feels, a significant ethical and professional commonality still emerges strongly from all this.

Counterpoints

Burawoy's schema has been widely hailed as immensely useful, getting near-unanimous support for his vigorous emphasis on public sociology: sociologists, we all agree, must be, and must be seen to be, 'out there' in the media and in social movements, talking about social justice, showing how their work connects, and reanimating the corridors of academia that can often appear to be too removed from the events of the day. In addition, the highlighting of public sociology allows us to reclaim or upgrade previously undervalued figures and the movements they helped give voice to – Du Bois, Gilman, Addams and others. Another definite plus is that critical sociologies are seen to have a constructive, not just a negative role. Postcolonialism and feminism, for example, would not have emerged as legitimate areas of university enquiry had it not been for intellectual struggles from the margins, consistently identifying ways in which white, male and Eurocentric inclinations continue to operate. And policy sociology too is agreed to have been given a rightfully higher status, since painstaking studies of an applied kind, and their assiduous implementation, can markedly improve the fabric of democratic (and post-democratic) social life. Lastly, Burawoy does not neglect to praise orthodox academic work, orientated around objectivity, accepting that it remains entirely central – sociology, after all, is not exactly the same thing as activism or policy-making.

Everyone, then, must surely be quite happy with the 'four sociologies' idea – right? Wrong. Objections have been made with regard to each of Burawoy's categories, and their supposed separateness, thus casting doubt upon the whole schema.

Public sociology

Burawoy applauds the activist public sociologist's lack of traditional 'disinterestedness'. But at what point does committed public sociology simply merge into ideological messaging? In a world of multiple publics and media circuses, that line becomes hard to draw, and Burawoy rather ducks this issue of how or even whether the line should be drawn. He also trusts that the various militant and competing public sociologies will somehow add up to a harmonious chorus singing for the good of humanity as a whole; but a more accurate image might be that of a cacophony of discordant versions of society and humanity. For example, it is hard to see, even in a post-secular age, religious social movement sociologists being naturally in tune with the claims and causes of unbelieving sociologists (and vice versa). And whilst Burawoy tends to draw his exemplary cases of public sociology from good left-liberal causes, nothing in the scheme itself rules out, say, fundamentalist, racist or conservative public sociologies.

Policy sociology

Burawoy respects policy sociology, but perhaps not enough. After all, there are probably more sociologists involved in that kind of work than are active in social movements. Another criticism here concerns post-disciplinarity. Burawoy refers to policy-related thinking as a branch of sociology but many researchers involved in such work would identify more with interdisciplinary subject areas like social policy and education. In fact, it is not clear why Burawoy's entire scheme is claimed specifically for sociology as such, when it might be better to think of it as applying to the social sciences as a whole. Coming from the opposite direction, it has also been maintained that there is no need for the category of policy sociology at all, because professional sociology has always contained policy-related sub-areas (sociology of crime, sociology of health, sociology of education and so on).

Professional sociology

Burawoy tries to uphold the strengths of professional sociology. But is he being honest with us? Of the four sociologies, it is professional sociology alone that comes in for negative comment and the hint comes across that, deep down, it is boring, morally complacent and positivistic. To reinforce this innuendo, Burawoy brackets policy and professional sociology together as 'instrumental' in orientation, with a slightly pejorative connotation, whereas public and critical sociology are set apart as intrinsically 'reflexive', a term of approval. But this seems tendentious. Sociology may well be academic, but its academic essence cannot be other than reflexive, questioning and open-ended. That is why it is also – arguably – intrinsically moral. When we study sociology, we are committed to finding out new things about the world, and testing all ideas to the full. This often has a liberating effect on us as persons, not least because as well as enabling us to challenge the dominant common sense, we are compelled to challenge our own common sense, too, our own unthinking prejudices. The conclusion to this response to Burawoy is therefore that professional sociology doesn't need a special branch of public sociology to encourage its students to get involved in the real world; nor does it need a special branch of critical sociology to ensure that assumptions and methods are routinely questioned. These things are all part of professional sociology's ongoing culture of rigorous evidence and argument.

Critical sociology

Burawoy portrays this branch as exclusively in the business of critiquing, of continually striving to outsmart and rumble the professional sociological establishment, grandstanding for 'emancipatory' alternatives. Ironically, though, this image makes critical sociology look like arrogant and elitist armchair philosophizing. Furthermore, Burawoy's presumption is that critical sociology is always to be found on the excluded margins of the discipline. Yet there are a great many staff in university sociology departments today who have come from the critical traditions, with many of those in the supposed establishment now regarding themselves as marginalized. Are they now the true critical sociologists?

One sociology, four tasks

Those reservations about Burawoy's schema are weighty, but no more completely decisive than his own arguments.

Improvising on Runciman (1983), perhaps we can look at the whole debate in a slightly different way. Perhaps there are not four different sociologies as such, practised by different sorts of people, but rather four different sorts of aspects or tasks.

One indispensable sociological task is to try to provide a basic description of the part of the social world that is under investigation, based on careful observation. It is often possible, after all, to agree that such and such happened, that he or she said what they did, and that a certain number of people in a certain setting are doing certain sorts of things. Without some kind of factual basis, sociology would just decline into opinion-swapping. Yet even if such evidential descriptions are possible, it is telling observations and insightful descriptions that really matter. So we always need to interpret the basic states of affairs; indeed interpretation is needed just to say which sorts of facts and situations are basic in the first place, and of what their 'basicness' consists.

The work of interpretation can take different forms, some of them attuned to the experiences and attitudes of the actual people whose lives are bound up in the situations described, and some more detached from the experiential level, taking shape as general explanations about the causes and functions of the phenomena in question. So we have at least three tasks here: description, interpretation and explanation. But we also generally want to express a view on whether whatever we are describing, interpreting and explaining is a good thing for society or not. And we generally have views about which interpretations and explanations are good and acceptable. This is the sociological task or aspect of evaluation, which is necessarily 'critical' in a general intellectual sense and quite often in a moral and political sense, too. In evaluating, we are striving to make cognitive judgements about how adequate a state of affairs or an explanation is; yet we are also adding or deriving our own values of one kind or another. In this way, the aspect of evaluation enters into the very framing of the other three tasks, so that our sequence is really a feedback loop: start anywhere in the cycle running from description through interpretation and explanation to critical evaluation and you will find yourself needing to come back to the others again. In fact, the cycle is really a spiral.

In sum

The four tasks depicted in that last section are no more easily separable from one another than Burawoy's four sociologies, but it does seem appropriate to distinguish them from one another. And, just like his schema, sociologists will diverge on which task is ultimately the most important. For example, as I write this, there is something of a campaign going on amongst social theorists to downgrade the aspect of explanation in favour of the aspect of description (and you might recall that both Spencer and Simmel had their own versions of this move). But maybe it is more convincing to hold that instead of any one aspect being regarded as decisively superior, and instead of there being four different types of sociologist, all sociologists continually juggle and interweave all four tasks in their thinking. That is the challenge, and the reward, of the study of social systems, institutions, interactions and ideologies.

Interchange

Question:

Come on, own up: what aspect of the fourfold sociological cycle do you stick up for most?

Response:

It's a fair question. Most people are temperamentally aligned with one or other of the modes of understanding rather than all of them in equal measure. On the other hand, it is an unmistakeable feature of twenty-first-century thinking right across the range of enquiry — whether in the humanities, the social sciences or the natural sciences — that no field of study can afford to do without all four dimensions. Perhaps this is what interdisciplinarity or post-disciplinarity is really all about. My own sense is that sociology ceases to have any distinctive identity if it does not underline the centrality of explanation. In due course you will come to develop your own considered preference. Take your time.

Next steps

In the interest of flow and graspability, this book almost completely lacks the apparatus of reference and citation that university teachers (rightly) demand from their students. The idea is that readers will quite naturally go on from this companion to study more extensive introductions to sociology, and more advanced engagements in social theory. As for textbooks and critical overviews, the following represent good next steps, especially for sociology students.

Mega-textbooks, for thorough introductory study

Abbott, P. and Wallace, C. (2006), *An Introduction to Sociology: Feminist Perspectives*, 3rd edition, London: Routledge.

Alexander, J.C. and Thompson, K. (2009), *A Contemporary Introduction to Sociology*, Boulder, CO: Paradigm Publishers.

Cohen, R. and Kennedy, P. (2007), *Global Sociology*, 2nd edition, Basingstoke: Palgrave.

Fulcher, J. and Scott, J. (2007), *Sociology*, 3rd edition, Oxford: Oxford University Press.

Giddens, A. (2006) *Sociology*, 5th edition, Cambridge: Polity Press.

Macionis, J. and Plummer, K. (2008), *Sociology: A Global Introduction*, 4th edition, Harlow: Prentice Hall.

Shorter introductions, clear and useful, but sometimes engagingly advanced, too

Abercrombie, N. (2004), *Sociology*, Cambridge: Polity Press.

Bauman, Z. and May, T. (2001), *Thinking Sociologically*, 2nd edition, Oxford: Blackwell.

Berger, P.L. (1963), *Invitation to Sociology: a Humanistic Perspective*, Garden City, NY: Anchor Books.

Bruce, S. (2000), *Sociology: A Very Short Introduction*, Oxford: Oxford University Press.

Crow, G. (2005), *The Art of Sociological Argument*, Basingstoke: Palgrave.

Evans, M.E. (2006), *A Short History of Society*, Maidenhead: Open University Press.

Fevre, R. and Bancroft, A. (2010), *Dead White Men and Other Important People*, Basingstoke: Palgrave.

Fuller, S. (2006), *The New Sociological Imagination*, London: Sage.

Jenkins, R. (2002), *Foundations of Sociology*, Basingstoke: Palgrave.

McLennan, G., McManus, R. and Spoonley, P. (2009), *Exploring Society: Sociology for New Zealand Students*, 3rd edition, Auckland: Pearson.

Matthewman, S., Lane West-Newman, C. and Curtis, B. (eds) (2007), *Being Sociological*, Basingstoke: Palgrave.

Mills, C.W. (1959), *The Sociological Imagination*, Oxford: Oxford University Press.

Parker, J., Ramsone, P.E., Stanworth, H.S. and Mars, L. (2003), *Social Theory: A Basic Tool Kit*, Basingstoke: Palgrave.

Runciman, W.G. (1998), *The Social Animal*, London: Harper Collins.

Higher undergraduate/postgraduate resources

Benton, T. and Craib, I. (2001), *Philosophy of Social Science*, Basingstoke: Palgrave.

Burnett, J., Jeffers, S. and Thomas, G. (eds), *New Social Connections: Sociology's Subjects and Objects*, Basingstoke: Palgrave.

Calhoun, C. (ed.) (2007), *Sociology in America: A History*, Chicago, IL: University of Chicago Press.

Calhoun, C., Gerteis, J., Moody, J., Pfaff, S. and Virk, I. (eds) (2007), *Contemporary Sociological Theory*, Oxford: Blackwell.

Calhoun, C., Gerteis, J., Moody, J., Pfaff, S. and Virk, I. (eds) (2007), *Classical Sociological Theory*, Oxford: Blackwell.

Callinicos, A. (2007), *Social Theory: An Historical Introduction*, 2nd edition, Cambridge: Polity Press.

Gordon, S. (1993), *The History and Philosophy of Social Sciences*, London: Routledge.

Hall, S., Held, D., Hubert, D. and Thompson, K. (eds) (1996), *Modernity: An Introduction to Modern Societies*, Oxford: Blackwell.

Harrington, A. (ed.) (2005), *Modern Social Theory: An Introduction*, Oxford: Oxford University Press.

Holmwood, J. (1996), *Founding Sociology? Talcott Parsons and the Idea of General Theory*, Harlow: Longman.

Hughes, J.A., Martin, P.J. and Sharrock, W.W. (2003), *Understanding Classical Sociology*, London: Sage.

Jackson, S. and Scott, S. (eds) (2002), *Gender: A Sociological Reader*, London: Routledge.

Lemert, C. (2004), *Social Theory: The Multicultural and Classic Readings*, 3rd edition, Boulder, CO: Westview Press.

Marshall, B.L. and Witz, A. (2004), *Engendering Social Theory*, Maidenhead: Open University Press.

McLennan, G. (2006), *Sociological Cultural Studies*, Basingstoke: Palgrave.

Oakley, A. (2000), *Experiments in Knowing: Gender and Method in the Social Sciences*, Cambridge: Polity Press.

Ritzer, G. (2008), *Modern Sociological Theory*, 7th edition, Boston, MA: McGraw-Hill.

Ritzer, G. and Smart, B. (eds) (2001), *Handbook of Social Theory*, London: Sage.

Rodriguez, E.G., Boatca, M. and Costa, S. (eds) (2010), *Decolonizing European Sociology*, Farnham: Ashgate.

Runciman, W.G. (1983), *A Treatise on Social Theory, Vol. 1, The Methodology of Social Theory*, Cambridge: Cambridge University Press.

Savage, M. and Burrows, R. (2007), 'The Coming Crisis of Empirical Sociology', *Sociology* 41: 5: 885–99.

Scott, J. (2006), *Social Theory: Central Issues in Sociology*, London: Sage.

Seidman, S. (2007), *Contested Knowledge: Social Theory Today*, 3rd edition, Oxford: Blackwell.

Sharrock, W.W., Hughes, J.A. and Martin, P.J. (2003), *Understanding Modern Sociology*, London: Sage.

Turner, D.C. (2010), *Investigating Social Theory*, London: Sage.

Index